On Your Own
in College

WILLIAM C. RESNICK
Wilbur Wright College
Chicago City College

DAVID H. HELLER
Loop College
Chicago City College

On Your Own in College

Second Edition

Charles E. Merrill Publishing Company
A Bell & Howell Company
Columbus, Ohio

Illustrations by MORRIE BRICKMAN

International Standard Book Number: 0-675-09517-4

Library of Congress Catalog Card Number: 72-76338

2 3 4 5 6 7 8 9 10—73 72 71 70

PRINTED IN THE UNITED STATES OF AMERICA

Preface

The freshman year in college is a time of searching, doubts, and confusion. It is also a time of discovery, decision, and accomplishment.

The purposes of this book are to help you, the freshman
—to gain a perspective on what it means to go to college today;
—to make the most of your college experiences by improving your study skills;
—to make practical use of recent research on learning and problem solving;
—to understand the life of your college community and to achieve a satisfying role for yourself within it.

Despite all the effort which has been made to prepare you for college, you may find yourself beset by surprises and faced by problems you feel unequipped to solve. Freshmen, typically, are too often bewildered by their new freedoms, appalled by a radical increase in work, disturbed by moral dilemmas, and upset by conflicting values. For some, the freshman year becomes a problem of sheer survival.

Although some degree of stress is inevitable and some may even be desirable, many of the frustrations freshmen undergo can be avoided by making use of the experiences of other freshmen. Their adjustments, their solutions, and their successes can help new freshmen to see college as a rewarding series of challenges rather than a dismal series of trials. There is another potential source of help for freshman—the research which has been done on students' problems. Even though our knowledge is far from complete, a great many recent findings can be applied today.

Properly used, then, this book can help you to develop self-understanding and self-direction. Its aim is not to lay down a rigid set of standards or a fixed plan; still less is it to preach or exhort. On the contrary, you are expected to carry on a dialogue with the book, argue with it, challenge it, modify it, and make it serve your own needs.

You yourself must furnish the effort, the time, and the enthusiasm which are indispensable for attaining success in college. This book will prove useful to you only if your own daily practices begin to reflect your own future goals.

For this second edition of *On Your Own in College* we have made changes in the organization of the chapters, have rewritten much of the text, and have brought the research up to date. Included is virtually the entire text of our *Learning Your Way Through College* (Columbus, Ohio: Charles E. Merrill Publishing Company, 1965). We have also, in response to many requests, added a chapter on the moral problems of students. Some new readings have also been included.

Our grateful thanks are due to the many students, colleagues and reviewers who received the first edition of this book so kindly.

Once again, we wish to thank our wives who again tried with a singular lack of success to keep from interrupting our work.

William C. Resnick
David H. Heller

Highland Park, Illinois
February, 1969

Acknowledgments

We are deeply indebted to our colleagues who generously helped us with criticisms and suggestions, to our students who have generally been very patient with us, and to the many college administrators and professors who were kind enough to respond to our requests for help.

Dr. Macklin Thomas of Chicago State College made a number of helpful suggestions for the improvement of Chapter 11.

Professor John N. Link, chairman of the Speech Department, Wilbur Wright College, Chicago, Illinois, wrote the section on speech in Chapter 9.

Professor George Hayes of the Loop College, Chicago, Illinois, contributed a portion of the section on literature in Chapter 9.

Professor Irwin Suloway of Chicago State College made some valuable suggestions on studying poetry for Chapter 9.

Professor Herbert H. Paper of the University of Michigan read and commented helpfully on the section concerning foreign languages in Chapter 9.

President Jerome Sachs, Northeastern Illinois State College, edited the section on mathematics in Chapter 10.

Professor Merlin Clark of Chicago State College originally wrote the section on social sciences in Chapter 10.

Chapter 8 is drawn in large part from a booklet by Professor Minnie Bowles Johnson of Chicago State College, first published as *Your Library Handbook* (Hampton, Virginia: Huntington Library, Hampton Institute, 1956).

Mrs. Katherine Byrne read and criticized the entire manuscript and her suggestions have been particularly valuable.

Parts of Chapters 2 and 19 are based on the comments of many college counselors and administrators. Among the most helpful were: Brother Jude Aloysius, Lewis College; Rudolph D. Anfinson, Eastern Illinois University; Frank C. Arnold, Bowling Green State University; Clarence J. Bakken, California State College (Long Beach); Bruce C. Barton, University of Hartford; Harold H. Betting, Lyons Township Junior College; Wheadon Block, University of Missouri (Kansas City);

John T. Bonner, Jr., The Ohio State University; Lester G. Brailey, Kent State University; Charles W. Brennan, Lehigh University; W. R. Brown, The University of Oklahoma; Alexander R. Cameron, The University of Rochester; J. Elliot Cameron; Brigham Young University; Harold B. Cochrane, Glendale College; Richard C. Devecchio, Freeport Community College; The Reverend Mel Doyle, Quincy College; John P. Dunlop, The University of Connecticut; Charles D. Ferguson, Parsons College; John P. Gwin, Beloit College; R.L. Hansford, The University of Akron; Elizabeth Hartshorn, Denison University; Noble Hendrix, University of Miami; John E. Hocutt, University of Delaware; Robert W. Hubbell, State University of Iowa; Richard W. Hulet, Illinois State University (Normal); Merrill E. Jarchow, Carleton College; C. Robert Keesey, University of New Hampshire; Mrs. Sally Taylor King, Bradford Junior College; David R. Knapp, Anchorage Community College; Larry L. Kroeker, Colorado State University; David E. Long, MacMurray College; Donald Loucks, The Florida State University; Ivan C. Malm, Fullerton Junior College; Edward C. McGuire, University of Rhode Island; Barbara Mertz, University of Denver; Leona S. Morris, Baltimore Junior College; Frank Naccarato, Morton Junior College; William G. Owen, University of Pennsylvania; Miss Marjorie Paisley, Montana State University; Mrs. Alyce Graham Pasca, Roosevelt University; Theodore K. Pierson, Phoenix College; Marie R. Prahl, Flint Community Junior College; Ralph E. Prusok, Kansas State University; Herbert F. Schwomeyer, Butler University; Merl F. Sloan, El Camino College; George H. Stanley, University of Bridgeport; Harold E. Stewart, Wayne State University; John Henry Stibbs, Tulane University; Herbert Stroup, Brooklyn College; John E. Tucker, D.S.A., Arkansas Polytechnic College; Fred H. Turner, University of Illinois; Charles Van Way, Jr., The American University; Fred J. Vogel, Northeast Louisiana State College; Laurence C. Woodruff, The University of Kansas; William McK. Wright, De Pauw University.

Contents

On Your Own
In College

PART 1

Going to College

Why Attend College?

What Can You Expect from College?

Are Freshmen Prepared for College?

What Are the Typical Problems of Freshmen?

CHAPTER 1

Why Attend College?

The influence of the college pervades American life. Newspapers and magazines feature columns about its peculiarities. Clothing stores offer "college fashions" for everyone, and college fads are eagerly adopted by hordes of teen-agers. A once distinctive college symbol, the cap and gown, has become the common attire for graduations at all levels down to and including the nursery school. Public interest and concern has mounted as the romantic image of college life is blurred by reports of widespread campus unrest and dissent.

Just attending college, even for a brief period of time, is regarded by some as a lasting source of social prestige. Throughout their lives, some adults talk about their "college days" even though, upon close examination, these days may have lasted only from registration until after the first quiz.

Never before in history has there been so much interest in the American college. Scholars analyze its motives, and researchers probe its structure. Organizations and foundations issue lengthy reports about college problems, and congressional committees hold hearings and introduce new educational legislation. High school students dream of going away to college, and parents, believing college to be a necessity of life, gird themselves for the financial sacrifices they must incur. Even infants in their cradles are now given insurance policies to guarantee that they will some day be able to pay their way through college.

Parents often have unrealistically high expectations about what a college can do for their child. Many well-meaning parents look upon college-going as indispensable, as the one important way to "get somewhere" and the chief means for social advancement. They may know little about what actually takes place in college and may, in fact, have little regard and appreciation for the intellectual way of life. Many parents expect college not only to prepare their child to earn a lucrative living and develop his mind, but also to be in the right social setting

---

Our colleges and universities represent our ultimate educational resource. In these institutions are produced the leaders and other trained persons whom we need to carry forward our highly developed civilization. If the colleges and universities fail to do their job, there is no substitute to fulfill their responsibility. The threat of opposing military and ideological forces in the world lends urgency to their task. But that task would exist in any case.

—John F. Kennedy

---

to develop his morals and introduce him to the "right" people. They are often surprised when their children return with disturbing new ideas.

In comparison with most of the rest of the world, the United States today enjoys a conspicuous prosperity, and its citizens have chosen to spend a significant portion of their wealth on the expansion of educational opportunity. Our affluent society no longer requires that almost every young person go to work as soon as he is physically able. The growth in technology has required an increase in the number of highly skilled personnel, but at the same time, there has been a marked decrease in the number of unskilled workers who are needed. Each year a college education becomes a requirement for greater numbers of jobs. One writer has even said that a college degree now makes the difference between those who can aspire to leadership in our society and those who cannot.

The national government has become ever more involved in higher education. It provides equipment and facilities to colleges as well as loans and scholarships to their students. Much of the research conducted in our universities is now financed by grants from federal agencies. It is clear that governmental support is playing an important part in the current growth of the colleges. President Johnson explained that "Better-informed, better-educated, more fully trained people are essential, not just to our national prosperity, but to the effective functioning of every facet of our free society (1)." On another occasion he said that a man with a grade school education earns an average of $152,000 in a lifetime, a high school graduate earns $272,000, while a college graduate averages $452,000.

As a result of all the reasons already mentioned, as well as such factors as the increase in total population, there has been an expansion of college enrollment in the United States which is literally without precedent.

> From a college and university enrollment of 1,500,000 in 1940, students in higher education increased to almost 2,700,000 in 1950, to 3,200,000 in 1960, and to 5,700,000 in 1965. It is projected that enrollment in colleges and universities will reach 7,000,000 by 1970, and 8,800,000 by 1980. Thus, enrollment in higher education will have almost tripled between 1950 and 1970.

> ...Whereas only 4.6 per cent of American adults had completed a college education in 1940, this proportion had increased to 7.6 per cent by 1960, and will have increased to 13 per cent by 1980 (2).

REASONS WHY STUDENTS ENROLL IN COLLEGE

Recently a number of college freshman were asked why they were attending college and what they hoped to gain from the experience. Although their underlying motivations are undoubtedly varied and complex, most of them gave several different reasons. These are classified and summarized below.

"Everybody expects me to go."

Many young men and women report that they feel a generally increased pressure for college attendance. They are made to believe that if they do not continue their education, all is lost. These impressions are reinforced through radio, television, and various publications. They are told that people without training cannot succeed in our highly technical society, that the future belongs to the educated man, that higher education is the ticket to opportunity. Teenagers, they say, repeatedly hear that college graduates make much more money, are better citizens, and lead more meaningful and useful lives.

> Why am I in college? Ask my parents. They're the ones who insist I go here.

> I don't really think I'm college material. I don't like studying. But they tell me anybody can profit from going. I hope they're right.

> All my friends are in college, so I figured I might as well go too.

"I want to be a doctor, or something."

For many, college is regarded primarily as the training ground for a specific vocational or professional goal. Such students want to get ahead as quickly as possible. They expect to become physicians, lawyers, teachers, businessmen or engineers. They are impatient with any courses that they feel are unrelated to their future job, or that are not specifically required by a graduate school.

> College is the only way to get into a profession. Graduates get the best jobs.

> My father is a CPA and built up a big business and he says it would be a shame if I don't share in it.

> What I want is a shingle of my own. After that, it's all gravy.

"I want to be somebody."

Students often look forward to success in terms of attaining a respected place in the community, a home and family of their own, and time and money for leisure activities. They seek the fuller life. Above all, they want to be safe in the world today. They are not sure just how to accomplish this, but they have faith that college will help them, in some way, to gain inner security, in addition to vocational training.

I want a position, not just a job. I want security in my later life.

Money counts and everyone knows that the difference between a college graduate and a dropout is a million dollars.

I want to be respected and college will show me how to handle people.

"I want to make good contacts."

It is commonly believed that social contacts made in college will be of great benefit, even though the modern college is increasingly hetero-geneous and impersonal; moreover, the mobility of society today makes it less likely that graduates will often see their former classmates. Some come to college to find a mate, and the rate of student marriages is increasing. It does remain true that college graduates marry other graduates.

College gives one an opportunity to develop friendships that will last a lifetime.

I'm not really looking for a husband now but there's no harm in being in the right place.

My father made a living for years just by selling insurance to his fellow alumni.

"I want to get educated."

Some students come to college in order to learn how to live *happier and more meaningful lives*. They believe that college will broaden them culturally, stimulate their minds, clarify their values, and open up a whole new intellectual world.

I'm here because I want to find out what it's all about.

College can bring you up from a superstitious bigot to a rational liberal.

By association with others pursuing intellectual growth, a student becomes aware of a world of thought beyond the typical "What shall I have for dinner tonight?" or "What's going to be on the Late Show?"

College can build one's mind. It can enlighten one to things he never knew existed.

"I want to grow up."

Students and their parents may look upon college as an important part of growing up. They expect that it will make children into adults, and produce basic changes in character and personality.

College is good preparation to help adjust to the responsibilities in life.

College should help me to mature in my opinions and values.

College can make a student more liberal and open-minded besides educating him at the same time. College can make an extrovert out of an introvert.

"I want to help people."

When parents of the present generation of students might have been attending college, it was popular to express a desire to improve society and to build a better world. In contrast, very few students in the present study went beyond their own personal concerns. Those who did display any altruism usually thought in terms of direct relationships rather than social movements.

I want to be a social worker so I can help delinquents.

As soon as I get out of college I will go into the Peace Corps and do some good for people.

I know what a maladjusted person goes through so I want to become a psychiatrist.

"I want to have a good time."

Campus social life is very important to many students, although very few in the current study mentioned it as a reason for attending college. Other research, perhaps more sophisticated, shows that social life ranked far higher than academic pursuits as a major interest of college freshmen (3).

I'm having a ball at college. I just wish I didn't have to go to classes.

I'm only nineteen and it's too early to get serious about anything.

You don't have to go looking for dates here, they're all buzzing around you.

"I don't know why I'm going."

Many students frankly admitted that they really did not know what they were doing in college and some said they were attending only because the alternatives were even worse.

College can keep a student out of the Army. It can also give him ulcers, nervousness, and an extreme case of poverty.

I've been in school since I was three. I don't know any other way of life.

I don't know what I really want to do. I never knew. I'm just marking time here.

THE PROBLEM OF COMPLETING COLLEGE

In recent years increasing attention is being paid to the large number of students who enter college but leave before completing their entire course. Almost half of all entering students now do this (4). There is, however, an increasing tendency for those who leave to return at a later time, either to the college they left or to another college. One investigator has remarked that "the only really permanent dropouts appear to be the deceased (5)."

No simple explanations are adequate to explain the large number of dropouts. Some students leave because they simply lack the ability to do college-level work. Such situations are most commonly found in state or community colleges which are required by law to admit all high school graduates. Other students with high academic potential leave because they do not fit into the intellectual way of life characteristic of their college. Some do not like the faculty. Others leave because they find the pressures too great—pressures which may come from their parents, the college, or from within themselves. Some drop out because they realize that they do not know what they want from life, and conclude that the college is not helping them. Other reasons given for leaving college are widely varied: illness, anxiety, military service, marriage or divorce, financial reasons, and many others.

Traditionally, college counselors tend to encourage students to resolve their problems without leaving college, but some now take the position that certain students may profit from withdrawal, at least temporarily. The students may go to work, or into military service, or join VISTA, or the Peace Corps, or transfer into an entirely different kind of college. Later, it is found that a large number of withdrawals actually do return to some college to complete their education.

RECENT TRENDS IN COLLEGES

Colleges are required to play new roles.

Until the second half of the nineteenth century college students concentrated on rhetoric, mathematics, Greek, Latin, and the history and literature of antiquity. Then the Industrial Revolution, which had transformed all of society, finally began to affect the colleges. Life today is increasingly complex, and our colleges have been required to become more complex to satisfy the needs of the society they serve. Many changes and additions have thus been made in the traditional college program.

The diversity that now characterizes higher education in the United States is unprecedented, and is incredible to foreign visitors. There is higher education for the extremely gifted and for the less gifted, for the future professor and the future tradesman. There is higher education with a strong theoretical bias, or with a strong practical bias. There is higher education in every kind of social and sociological context—urban or rural, religious or secular (6).

This great diversity of goals has produced widespread changes in curriculum. James B. Conant tells us, "In the last fifty years, the number of undergraduate professional or semi-professional programs has increased greatly. For example, journalism, home economics, business and commerce have all become accepted subjects for undergraduate study in at least some universities (7)." New fields of study are continually being added, and over 1600 different kinds of academic degrees are currently available in the United States.

Many colleges which were founded for a particular purpose or designed to attract one type of learner have expanded their course offerings and opened their doors to a wider diversity of students. Normal schools, for example, were converted into normal colleges and then into teachers colleges. These have been further transformed into liberal arts colleges and universities. Agricultural colleges have been similarly expanded into universities which offer a wide range of professional and liberal arts studies. Colleges which formerly were restricted to certain social classes and certain geographical areas may now deliberately set out to attract a more varied student body. Similarly, religious and ethnic

colleges have, in many cases, broadened their purposes and have attracted a new group of students. Colleges for women have also undergone a transformation, and many of them work more closely with
what were formerly colleges for men (8).

American colleges thus sometimes find themselves attempting to
serve functions which may be not only diverse but actually contradictory. At the same time they must cope with an ever-increasing number
of applicants for admission—applicants who vary widely in their preparation, goals, attitudes, and abilities

New kinds of students attend colleges.

Much of the increase in the college population is due to the enrollment
of new kinds of students. The traditional image of the American college student is that he is a young man, unmarried, carefree, middle or
upper class, white, and supported by his family, but every one of these
characteristics has begun to lose validity and the image is fading fast.

In reality, many students today receive little financial assistance from
their relatives; a few even have to help support their families while they
attend college. Requirements for admission are generally higher now
than ever before, and academic standards have risen. Instead of being
happy and carefree, the average college student today is more apt to
find himself under great pressures of all kinds, frequently confronted
by situations in which choices must be made that he feels unprepared
to make.

Professional programs have increased the length of time required in
college. About three-fourths of college seniors say they intend to attend
graduate schools (9). The average age of students has thus continued to
increase, and only half the students in colleges and universities today
are between 18 and 21 years old. Among the older students are those
who return after having been away from school, those who want to keep
up with the latest developments, and those who change to new fields of
study.

Although men still outnumber women in most colleges, there has been
a steady increase in the proportion of women until they now number
about one-third of the college population. Whereas in 1900 men
graduating from college outnumbered women by four to one, the gap
today is even closer than three to one (10). College women today earn
approximately one in every three B.A.'s and M.A.'s awarded and one
in every ten Ph.D. degrees. Generally, however, men stay longer for
advanced professional studies.

In the past, many girls who went to college had a missionary zeal for the emancipation of women. They wanted to enter vocations formerly reserved for men and to prove that they were equal to men. Today, for many girls, marriage and a family are the foremost goals—going to college is important not merely to provide opportunities to meet young men, but to help insure that their intellectual and cultural interests will be compatible with those of the college graduate they hope to marry. A college education is also looked upon by many woman as economic protection, in case they are unsuccessful in finding a suitable mate, or in case they wish to go to work after they have married and raised a family.

Before World War II there were few married students on campus. Those who did marry usually kept the fact a secret from college authorities, since marriage was considered grounds for dismissal on many campuses. Today, however, for better or worse, love has found a way, and married undergraduates are a much more familiar sight on campus than they were in their parent's time. A number of colleges now provide apartments for married students and some even provide nursery accommodations for their offspring.

Many more nonwhite students are enrolled in colleges today than previously. The migration of southern Negroes to the northern urban centers has increased their numbers in northern schools. As their standard of living and level of aspiration rise, more nonwhites want to attend college. Concurrently, there are greater job opportunities for these students. "Closing the doors of educational opportunity to any young person because of race, creed, origin or sex is . . . intolerable under the democratic principles upon which the United States is founded," declared a presidential committee (11).

Having discussed some reasons why students attend college and having surveyed a few of the recent changes in the colleges, we will consider in Chapter 2 what a student can expect from his college experience.

NOTES TO CHAPTER 1

(1)   Lyndon B. Johnson to the Nineteenth National Conference on Higher Education, April, 1964.
(2)   Phillip M. Hauser, "The Challenge of the Population Explosion and Implosion," *Illinois Education*, LIV, 8 (April, 1966), p. 363.
(3)   Henry Chauncey, Private Communication.
(4)   Robert E. Iffert, "The College Dropout and Talent Utilization," *School and Society*, XCIII, 2257 (March 6, 1965), pp. 163, 165.

(5)   Dorothy M. Knoell, *ibid.*, p. 165.

(6)   James B. Conant, *Slums and Suburbs* (New York: McGraw-Hill Book Co., 1961), p. 86.

(7)   *Ibid.*

(8)   In 1962, Radcliffe graduates were formally awarded Harvard degrees for the first time. Yale announced in 1968 that women would be admitted as regular students.

(9)   *Time*, LXXXVII, 15 (April 15, 1966), p. 82. The 314,000 graduate students. in the United States in 1960 had grown to 510,000 in 1966. By 1970 according to one estimate there will be about 800,000 graduate students.

(10) *United States Book of Facts, Statistics and Information* (New York: Pocket Books, Inc., 1965), based on data from the *Statistical Abstract of the United States* (Washington, D.C.: U.S. Government Printing Office, 1965).

(11) *President's Committee on Higher Education, Second Report* (1963), p. 8.

SUGGESTIONS FOR FURTHER READING

Barzun, Jacques, *The House of Intellect.* New York: Harper and Row, 1959.

Bell, Norman T., and others, *Introduction to College Life* (2nd ed.). New York: Houghton Mifflin Co., 1966.

Boroff, David, *Campus U.S.A.* New York: Harper and Row, 1962.

Brown, Judy, *What I Wish I Knew Before I Went to College.* New York: Pocket Books, 1966.

Dennis, L.E. and J.F. Kauffman (ed.)., *College and the Student.* Washington, D.C.: American Council on Education, 1966.

Garrison, Roger H., *The Adventure of Learning in College.* New York: Harper and Row, 1959.

Keats, John, *Sheepskin Psychosis.* New York: Dell Books, 1966.

Lloyd-Jones, Esther M., and H.A. Estrin, *American Student and His College.* New York: Houghton Mifflin Co., 1967.

Sanford, Nevitt, *College and Character.* New York: John Wiley and Sons, Inc., 1964.

Soldwedel, Bette J., *Mastering the College Challenge.* New York: The Macmillan Co., 1964.

VIEWPOINT

The American Idea
BY HAROLD TAYLOR

*What are the two fundamental weaknesses in our society,
according to Dr. Taylor?*
Are the main issues of modern life practical or theoretical?
*How does the American concept of education differ from
the European?*
*Is there a conflict between vocational training and liberal
education?*
*How important is college education to the American
Idea?* °

There are two fundamental weaknesses in contemporary American society, a lack of purpose and an over-concern with security. The two weaknesses are directly related to each other and mark a degeneration of American democratic philosophy into a doctrine of hedonism and *laissez-faire*. Where everything successful is approved, each must decide upon his own satisfactions and his own obligations, and, as Mill says, men "addict themselves to inferior pleasures, not because they deliberately prefer them, but because they are either the only ones to which they have access, or the only ones which they are any longer capable of enjoying." In the absence of constraint, and, as of late, in the absence of leadership, the personal choice of the citizen is conditioned more by what is convenient and materially gratifying than by what is honest, good and true.

In place of the bold line of progressive thinking, we are content to forsake our own tradition and to establish, without thought, an equilibrium of economic and political forces by simply allowing events to happen as they please and accommodating ourselves to their results. We therefore find ourselves alternately amazed and alarmed as we move from one crisis to the next with improvised policies to meet each one as it comes along . . .

Nowhere is this seen more clearly than in our public debates on education. Yet these very debates reflect the aimlessness of our national policy, the same impulsive jumps from crisis to crisis, the same tendency to run from problems and talk in empty abstractions, the same refusal to come to terms with the real issues of the world of the twentieth century.

Dr. Harold Taylor was formerly president of Sarah Lawrence College. This viewpoint was first published in *Current Issues in Higher Education* (Washington, D.C.: Association for Higher Education, 1960). Reprinted by permission.
° Questions preceding each "viewpoint" were provided by Resnick and Heller.

The real issues are not ideological. They are practical, and they have to do with establishing means of disarmament, feeding the hungry, teaching the ignorant, building schools, housing the destitute, giving productive work to the unemployed, using science for human welfare, and doing all these things on a world scale at a time when the Soviet Union is doing everything in its power to make our answers to these questions seem ineffective and their own unbeatable.

On the other hand, we do have a philosophy which lies at the heart of our social system, one which not only provides the working plan for a system of government, but which provides the moral and social energy which has made this country great. It has taught us how to deal with practical issues, how to establish a society based on justice, generosity of spirit, equality and mutual respect. It is a progressive philosophy which broke with the social ideas of the old world and set itself the task of building a new society on truly equalitarian lines. It is pragmatic, experimental, empirical, evolutionary, pluralistic, liberal, and democratic. Emerson was giving it a voice when he asked his famous question, "If there is any period one would desire to be born in, is it not the age of Revolution? When the old and the new stand side by side and admit of being compared; when the energies of all men are searched by fear and hope; when the historic glories of the old can be compensated by the rich possibilities of the new era?"

This is the authentic sound of America. I suggest that we return to our roots in the American tradition and enjoy the possibilities of the new era. I suggest that the optimism of progressive thought is at the center of American achievement, and the old and the new do stand side by side and do admit of being compared. When we compare them we can be proud of the fact that we have a national system of free and democratic education, free from authoritarian control either by church or state, operated by our citizens, and dedicated not only to the intellectual development of American youth, but to their moral and social welfare. We can be proud that this system has invented new forms of education previously unknown in Europe or anywhere else and that it stands as a monument to the democratic ideals of a new society founded in a new world.

There are those who now tell us that progressive philosophy in social and educational matters has weakened our society, that we must turn back to conservative doctrines as we enter the new era. The first thing we must do in education, we are told, is to return to European concepts, separate the sheep from the goats at an earlier age, put some to work with their hands, the other with their heads, select the gifted, stiffen the examinations, raise the requirements, stop trying to educate the whole man and the whole country and concentrate on the intellect and those who possess it.

But what then is our national aim in education? To compete with the Russians on their terms? It is clearly not this. It is to give to every child the education his talents deserve. The purpose in doing that is to open up his life to everything that is possible in the world, and thus to allow him to add his gifts to the total life of his community.

This philosophy is strong, active and understood among educators. When we say we mean to educate all American youth, we mean just that and nothing less. All American youth are not the same; they vary in talent, motivation and interest; some of them are poor, others rich; some of them city boys, others from the country; some of them are quick to learn, others slow; some of them are boys, some are girls. The progressive idea is to build an education which takes account of who the children are and what they can become. If they are ignorant, what they need is knowledge, not exclusion from further education; if they have not yet learned to learn, if their environment has crushed their curiosity, if they are culturally undernourished, if their vocabulary is underdeveloped, what they need is teaching which is lively, vigorous, informed and productive; they need a chance to get started, not more hours of textbook material which they can't yet handle. If their test scores are low, what they need is a teacher who can find out why and can set about raising them, not someone who classifies them as stupid on the basis of circumstantial evidence. If their teachers are incompetent what they need is better teaching, not a storm of rhetoric against American education.

The progressive says, education is for everyone; let us have all the students in our colleges who can qualify, let us seek them out. Let us use our universities to raise higher the level of intelligence of our whole population, not looking down at them from a height as if the educated minority were a separate breed possessing the innate virtues of the higher learning.

The progressive says, they are better than you think. The conservative says, they aren't what they should be. The progressive says, the child is at a stage in his development, give him a chance to grow; the conservative says, he's not good enough to be promoted. The progressive says, human nature is malleable, mankind is perfectible; the conservative says, human nature is everywhere the same, afflicted with sloth and original sin.

Progressive philosophy rejects, as a start, the idea that there are two separate realms, the mind and the body, one for thought and another for action, one for the liberal arts, another for science and the vocations, or that the intellectual and the ordinary citizen live in different worlds.

To be specific, the philosophy which I am advocating is the philosophy of those practical-minded democrats who founded the state universities not as sanctuaries for the liberal arts nor as the special preserve of intellectuals, but as institutions of learning which could meet the needs of the people of the state. The natural sciences were obviously important since they provided the knowledge on which agriculture, industry and the expansion of modern society rested; the social sciences were important because they gave to the people the facts and the insight by which the state could write its tax bills, organize its social welfare, build its communities; the arts were important because they fulfilled the need of the people for experience with aesthetic and cultural values in their daily lives.

For the student with a purpose, at a university which recognizes what that purpose is, there can be no conflict between vocational training and liberal education. The curriculum will contain those studies and will foster those experiences which are significant in the individual lives of the students and are at the same time relevant to the needs of society in which the students will live.

Some of them will be scientists, others lawyers, others businessmen, others nurses, teachers, dietitians, doctors, salesmen, farmers. But if their university education has been successful they will be prepared to take the role in society for which their talents are best suited, and they will at the same time be liberally educated, that is to say, they will be interested in the arts, in ideas, in thinking critically and creatively about their society, in forming standards of taste and of judgment about the culture which surrounds them.

We must rescue the idea of *vocation* from the disrepute into which it has fallen and the misuse to which it has been put. Training in the techniques of fly-fishing, basketball playing, business practice, radio repair or personal charm is not the responsibility of the scholars and teachers of a university. Such training where needed can best be given in institutions designed for that purpose, and we need make no apology for such institutions if they do what they are intended to do. On the other hand, the essence of the liberal arts is not that they are nonvocational. They are directly related to one's vocation. A vocation is a calling, something to which the individual is drawn by talent and interest, something to which he is called. The liberal arts furnish the forms of experience through which the individual can learn to make discriminating judgments about himself and his world, and the truly educated man is one who has learned to use what he has in ways which are productive both to himself and to his society.

It is for this reason that the progressive philosophy advocates the fusion of the liberal and the vocational, the practical and the theoretical, in one curriculum. It puts its emphasis on the practice of the creative arts rather than on textbooks about them, but in so doing does not intend to ignore the study of those works of art which are classics in history. Similarly, a progressive philosophy urges the use of contemporary materials in the curriculum of politics and social studies, the use of direct experience with political and social phenomena, but not at the expense of the wider views to be obtained through the study of history and the literature of the past.

How then is education related to the national purpose? What do we have to do with establishing a national purpose? Certainly we must take account of the national need for scientists, engineers, linguists, and skilled workers of all kinds to strengthen the national defense. Certainly we must improve the range and quality of the high school curriculum by enriching the content of our courses in science, mathematics, history and languages. The students are ready for it whenever we are.

But the purpose in doing so is not merely to maintain American prosperity and military security by recruiting technically trained manpower. The national purpose is to establish a just and peaceful world order in which we as the greatest democratic power take the leadership in democracy. We therefore need to concentrate our national attention on the proposition that a free society in a free world can only be achieved when our educational system has not only taught its citizens the skills and techniques necessary to run a modern industrial society, but has taught them to believe in the generosity of heart, the boldness of imagination and the liberal ideals of a truly democratic philosophy.

VIEWPOINT

The College Student and the Idea of Learning

BY ERNEST HAVEMANN

Which are more adaptable—intellectuals or nonintellectuals?

Do college freshmen want to become intellectuals?

Do our "best homes" provide better cultural opportunities?

Why don't the American colleges produce more intellectuals?

Does Havemann agree with Taylor about the purpose of going to college today?

Last summer . . . there was a full-page advertisement in the New York City newspapers which showed a man who was obviously an intellectual. I forget whether the photographer had equipped him with a Phi Beta Kappa key, or a mortar-board, or horn-rimmed glasses—but at any rate, you could see at a glance that the man was unusually brainy. Now the ad, strangely enough, and the headline on the ad said, "Even the intelligentsia read Dick Tracy."

Well, I have no quarrel with the ad. Intellectuals do read the comic pages—and this is a very important fact.

The intellectual, you see, is the most adaptable person in our society . . . All of us have highly intellectual friends who are great devotees of the comics or of jazz music, bull fighting, contract bridge, golf, detective stories, and primitive art—none of which is really an intellectual pursuit in any sense of the word. Moreover, intellectuals spend a good part of their days in nonintellectual activities such as cooking meals . . . or rearing children, mowing lawns, and driving their automobiles to and from work. Indeed many intellectuals earn their living at nonintellectual jobs . . . I am not sure that even teaching college freshmen is an intellectual occupation . . . .

When the intellectual and the nonintellectual meet socially . . . it is the intellectual who adapts to the situation and who talks about things like the weather and the sports page and the superficial aspects of politics that the others can understand. The interests of the nonintellectual prevail.

Dr. Havemann is a widely known author and lecturer. This viewpoint is addressed to college professors and is drawn from *Orientation to College Learning—A Reappraisal*, Nicholas C. Brown, ed. (Washington, D.C.: American Council on Education, 1961), pp. 103-113, as abstracted in *What the Colleges Are Doing*, Ginn and Company No. 120, Winter 1962, pp. 1, 6. Reprinted by permission.

... I hope to impress upon you what a difficult job you undertake when you try to introduce the new college student ... to intellectuality. You are trying to move against our society's main stream of traffic.

Let us consider for a moment what the student who arrives on the campus is really like. Let us permit ourselves to dream happy thoughts and assume that all the new arrivals are the offspring of America's finest families, with fathers both rich and famous. The College Board scores show that they have a great deal of intelligence, a considerable aptitude for both verbal thinking and mathematical concepts ... Does this mean that they arrive on the campus with a thirst for knowledge, eager for education, determined to be an intellectual? Some of our educators have assumed so over the years. They could hardly have been more wrong.

Twenty-five years in the practice of journalism have brought to me ... an opportunity to view a wide range of the American scene. My observations over that period do not, let me say candidly, give me much hope for the future of intellectuality. ...

I recall the mansion of an industrialist, a man who, incidentally, has served on several government commissions, and has quite a reputation for statesmanship. This was a truly beautiful country mansion with an outdoor swimming pool, bath-house, and innumerable cottages for servants and guests. In the main part of the house, not a single book. In my guest-room, when I retired, a single volume provided for such guests as might prove to be intellectual—Edgar Guest's poems. ...

Our "best" homes do not incline their children to intellectual pathways, and our wealthiest social groups favor skeet over Shakespeare and horsemanship over Horace Mann.

And now, just in case I haven't already discouraged you enough, let me talk briefly to you of another of the very serious problems which you face. This is the fact that the college freshman, alas and alack, is eighteen years old. ...

It takes a long time for the human brain to develop to its fullest capacity. ... Boys and girls of high school age are sufficiently mature to win Olympic medals in athletics. They are also sufficiently mature ... to marry and have children. But at what age do boys and girls become able really to appreciate a writer like Shakespeare or a teacher like Socrates? ... The very brightest boys and girls might achieve some sort of intellectual capacity at fourteen or fifteen. ... The average boy or girl who is going on to college would not have this ability until the age of seventeen or eighteen.

... This means ... that when these boys and girls arrive at the college campus, most of them are just beginning to possess the ability to think. Yet during the period when their brains were growing up, life went on. We didn't just keep them in cold storage for those eighteen years. They were alive and kicking all that time, and learning too. We adults, who especially in America devote tremendous amounts of time and money to our children, set up activities to keep them busy and to teach them.

... The schoolboy becomes a boy scout and learns that a man's worth is measured by his ability to start a fire without matches and make a bed of pine boughs . . . . For most of the eighteen years of his life before college, [we] are stuffing him full of the importance of athletics, outdoorsmanship, and the basic box step . . . .

Your beginning freshman not only comes to you ninety-nine times out of a hundred from a home and from a social background where the role of the intellect has been minimized, but also comes to you with a mind and character shaped by from fifteen to eighteen years of active life lived while his mind was quite immature. Intellectually speaking, these freshmen are babes in arms . . . .

It is because of our failure to admit this fact, I think . . . that American education has been a failure in the past. For I believe we have to admit that American education has been a failure. At least it has been a failure in terms of what it might have accomplished. In no other country, at no time in history, has such a high proportion of a nation's youth been privileged to receive so much education. This means that we have had an unprecedented opportunity to build an intellectual society—to take all the fine minds that would have gone uncultivated in other nations and in other times, and to start them marching up the high road to the mountains of pure reason . . . Thus, we live today in a nation which, according to the latest census report, has eight million college graduates, an unprecedented number, and millions more who have had part of a college education . . . . Yet surely no one could claim that we live in an intellectual climate . . . .

Why is this? Well, as I see it, there can be only one possible reason. The reason is very simple. The colleges of America have been content to produce an inferior intellectual product . . . .

We have attempted to set our students down in the classrooms, throw a certain number of facts at them, and then judge them by how many of the facts stick—often measuring this by a true-false test . . . A true-false test is perhaps the ultimate in academic bureaucracy. For in these tests we abandon all pretense of setting our own standards for our graduates. We let them set their own standards. When ten students sit down and take one of the tests—at least this was the formula in my day—the bottom one was flunked and the top one was elected to Phi Beta Kappa. It did not matter a bit whether they were all Einsteins or all near morons . . . We taught them and judged them by formula, and spared ourselves the wear and tear of thinking. We failed to guide them; we did not really try to make intellectuals out of them . . . .

o   o   o

The American educational philosophy has taken some strange twists and turns in the past. At one time we were classicists, who thought that if we taught a boy and girl—no, we did not even try to teach girls in those days—if we taught a boy sufficient Latin and Greek he would forever thereafter be able to solve all the intellectual problems with which he was confronted, including, presumably, the problem of how to live with a wife who had never studied either of those languages. More recently we have gone through a period when we were extreme pragmatists, and when many schools seemed to think they could fulfill their intellectual duty to civilization by teaching physical education and basket weaving. We know now from sad experience that both these philosophies were failures.

. . . Some of you, thank heaven, know why. You . . . have come to realize that the student who comes to your campus is not some preformed seedling easily and happily purchased from some mail-order house, which you can simply plant in a well-ventilated, well-fertilized, and well-watered library and watch grow . . . into a fully developed and complete intellectual. You know that, on the contrary, the student is simply a human being, from an all-too-human background, and that, besides this, he is pathetically and almost hopelessly young. He is not a seedling at all. Being much more complicated than any form of vegetable life, he is more like some exotic and very delicate egg, which must be fussed over, handled gently yet firmly, and kept at exactly the right temperature for the exact number of days. It isn't easy to hatch an intellectual. If it were, we should have hatched a lot more of them in the past. But it is among the world's most noble tasks, if also among the most difficult, and if you succeed at it you will have been the foster parents of a far brighter world than the one in which we live today.

VIEWPOINT

The University in Contemporary Society

BY GRAYSON KIRK

*What are the major differences between higher education
today and higher education of the past?*
*What are the major conflicting views as to the role of the
university today?*
*What does President Kirk think should be the role of the
university?*
What is the primary responsibility of the student?

There was a time, and not long ago, when in many countries higher education was by no means at the center of national life. It offered preparation for a
few professions, principally the ministry, and a gloss of classical culture to a
small elite of young men drawn largely from the more aristocratic segments of
society. It was often derided even by those who had sampled its wares. Carlyle
had his imaginary Prof. Teufelsdröckh speak of a university in which "the
young vacant mind [was] furnished with much talk about Progress of the Spe-
cies, Dark Ages, Prejudice and the like; so that all were quickly enough blown
into a state of windy argumentativeness; whereby the better sort had soon to
end in sick, impotent Scepticism; the worser sort explode in finished self-con-
ceit, and to all spiritual interests become dead." Gibbon referred to his time at
Magdalen College as "the most idle and unprofitable of my whole life." Max
Beerbohm once wrote, "I was a modest, good-humoured boy. It is Oxford that
has made me insufferable."

Today, higher education has a different place in the world. In this country we
are familiar with the changes wrought by the land-grant college concept, which
made university education more practical and more widely available. We are
equally aware of the fact that our borrowings from the great German university
system of the past century provided us for the first time with the concept of a
true university based upon advanced teaching and research. From the British
model of the residential college, the German university, and our own additions
we have developed a vast and complex array of higher educational institutions
with an aggregate annual expenditure for capital and operating costs of more
than $9,000,000,000 and with a total enrollment of more than 4,000,000 young
men and women.

Based on a commencement address by Dr. Kirk, former president of Columbia University, June, 1965, as reported in *School and Society,* (February 1, 1966). By permission.

In this tremendous development, the U.S. has been a part of a world-wide trend that continues to accelerate as governments struggle to meet the needs of a growing population. It is a trend that places an ever-higher valuation upon higher education. Thus, in our day, the university has become one of society's most cherished institutions. It is everywhere regarded as the principal agency whereby a country may protect its future as well as its past. It has become the one indispensable source for trained leadership for almost every segment of a modern society. Access to higher education now is regarded as the right of all young people who have any claim to intellectual promise—and is demanded by many who have not. Throughout the world, in countries old and young, powerful and weak, authoritarian and democratic, new universities are rising to meet a seemingly inexhaustible demand for higher education. In short, for the first time in history the university finds itself at the very center and heart of society. The university of today is large, extremely diverse in its activities, very expensive, and very important.

This new eminence is gratifying, even exhilarating, but it has its hazards as well as its benefits. University leaders nowadays seldom are free from involvement in some public controversy. They must manage what is in reality a large business enterprise, but one that is dedicated to non-business purposes, and they must do so in a way that will be acceptable to four different publics: the students, the faculty, the alumni, and that portion of the general public which on occasion is more lavish with its criticism than with its support. Academic administration usually is disliked by the students, viewed with suspicion by the faculty, and castigated by the public for not exercising an omnipotence that, in fact, it does not, and should not, possess.

But this is merely a detail of a larger picture. Because the university today is the agency wherein virtually all our leaders are trained—or at least profoundly influenced in their attitudes—society has a mounting concern over what goes on in the university. Efforts to express that concern inevitably affect the life of the university—and possibly the longevity of university administrators.

Some individuals and groups, responding to this new feeling of concern, seek to dominate the atmosphere of the university so as to ensure that its prime function will be to defend and protect traditional and declared national beliefs, values, and attitudes, and to inculcate them in the youth of each generation. They are not concerned about research or scholarship. They view the university as a guardian, not as an innovator, an instrument to transmit to youth the heroic past of the nation, its special culture, and its ideals. When a university goes beyond this, these groups are quick to rise up in condemnation and criticism. They feel that they have been betrayed.

Such a view finds fullest policy expression in any rigidly authoritarian state. There the university is merely an arm of the government, dutifully teaching an official ideology and carefully controlling student access to all contrary views or theories. Both *Lehrfreiheit°* *and Lernfreiheit†* are non-existent. In other coun-

---

° Freedom of the teacher to teach.
† Freedom of the student to learn.

tries where universities are more free, but still are wholly financed by and under the official control of a ministry of education, academic authorities often find it prudent to be extremely cautious about curricular innovations that might evoke controversy or arouse official displeasure. Thus, for example, the teaching of political science, as we know it, is almost non-existent in Latin American universities.

In most free countries, other groups seek to gain dominance over the university, not to protect an ideological, political, or social status quo, but to destroy it, or at least to erode the foundations upon which it rests. These groups believe that the essential function of a university is to be the fountainhead of social, economic, and political reform, and they are determined to direct its official life to that end. This view of a university's role is widely prevalent in Latin American academic circles.

For all activists who seek drastic social change, the university is an obvious target and a potential instrument of the greatest value. It is filled with young people whose natural idealism is as yet untempered by the patience and tolerance of maturity. These students are at a time of life when a normal feeling of revulsion against all authority easily can be diverted into violent antagonism toward existing political and economic institutions and policies. With the exuberant enthusiasm of youth, they are eager to find that Utopia that somehow all their elders have failed to discover. They may have studied history but they do not quite believe in it.

Moreover, the view that a university should be dedicated to social reform is not confined on campus to student leaders and their followers. Every university has many faculty members who by temperament and conviction are critics and reformists. They are not partisans for other ideologies or political systems, but some are restless under what they regard as the follies and the stupidities of their leaders. Nowhere else in society can such a group be as free to indulge in so much social criticism with complete immunity against any possible reprisal. This is as it should be; it is an invaluable asset to the university and to society, and it must be defended, even by a university president to whom complaints come from all those who believe they have been the victims of the slings and arrows of outrageous faculty criticism. Nonetheless, and despite the fact that it is indispensable to the life of a university, the existence of this group on every campus does enhance the potential attractiveness of the university in the eyes of those outsiders who would like to use it as an instrument to help them achieve their doctrinaire ends.

o   o   o

As we resist these efforts to make of the university either a bulwark of defense or an instrumentality of drastic change, we never must cease to proclaim to all concerned that the true and unchanging role of the institution is to be an open forum for *all* ideas and *all* opinions. The one eternal goal of a university is to foster the search for truth, however elusive it may be. We make progress toward that goal only as we encourage the fullest freedom of discussion on all matters which divide mankind into contending groups. If we fail to do this, we never will give to our students that quality of intellectual maturity that will enable them to become effective leaders and participants in an evolving democratic society. If we limit or constrain full freedom of discussion on any economic or political issue, we indicate thereby that we are unsure of the strength or validity of our own beliefs.

But, if the university is to maintain its independence and resist all assaults against its integrity, then it must keep its own house in order. Because it is so important to the health and vigor of contemporary society, the university of our time has a greater degree of public responsibility than in those days when it was content to inhabit a pleasant sanctuary of social unconcern.

This new responsibility runs throughout the institution. The modern university must seek consciously to hold and to deserve public confidence in the excellence of its work and the integrity of its purpose. Upon *all* members of the university community, therefore, there must be self-imposed *restraints* as well as asserted and recognized *rights*. These restraints cannot be imposed by any administration. But, unless they are recognized and observed, the university can ill defend itself against its critics or its would-be captors.

A scholar has an implied professional commitment to approach all issues more in the spirit of a judge than that of an advocate. He has an obligation, in Sir Walter Moberly's words, to be "doubly watchful and critical of the unconscious operation on his mind of his own pet prejudices and sympathies . . . an obligation more easily acknowledged than observed." When a scholar fails to keep this admonition in mind, in the long run he puts in danger the public acceptance of the essential integrity of the university.

The university student also has a primary responsibility, one that is a part of his right to his intellectual freedom. This is the obligation to yield to the views of others that respect he demands for his own. He may argue heatedly with his comrades the long night through, but he may not in good conscience attempt to interfere forcibly either with their free expression of differing views or with the activities that derive therefrom. A student who is unwilling to live by the simple rules of courtesy, decency, and good manners that govern an academic community has no proper place in it, and he should be invited to take himself elsewhere. The right to interfere with the rights of others is no part of academic freedom.

A democratic society can exist in a state of health only if all citizens observe a decent measure of courtesy and self-restraint in their dealings with others. This does not mean that one should be supine in the face of something that is believed to be dangerous or evil, but it does mean that one must attack it through those devices and procedures developed by society for the peaceful settlement of issues. Sir Walter Moberly also wrote that "An honest intention to fight the Lord's battles is no guarantee against mistaken objectives or illegitimate methods of warfare."

Moreover, we live in a world in which the communications gap between expert and layman steadily widens. This is of little relative importance in scientific or technical fields because the layman seldom undertakes to argue with the expert; he is acutely aware of what he does not know, and he is content to listen to those who do. But in the equally complex fields of public policy, there is no such self-restraint and the layman frequently proclaims that his opinion is just as valuable as that of a man who may have spent years in the study of the problem in question and who has at hand information which may not be generally available to the private citizen.

This is a source of possible danger to a democratic society in a complex world. Any layman has a citizen's right to disagree with policy decisions reached by his public officials, but he ought to hesitate before he asserts that his own view, which may be little more than a visceral, emotional reaction, is just as valid as that held by those who may have lived with the problem for a long time, who have access to all sources of information, and who have the responsibility for the consequences of the decision they have reached. Wisdom consists of knowing what one does not know quite as much as of knowing what one does know. Our graduates should have the sophistication of intellect to recognize the difference between the two.

CHAPTER 2

What Can You Expect from College?

The aims of college are, after all, abstract ideals; they are not destined to be fully realized in any individual student. The aims and attitudes which you as a student bring with you may weigh more heavily in deciding what you get out of the college experience than the aims of the college itself. As we have seen, some students come to college with a single objective: to learn skills for a particular occupation, or to "live it up," or to meet the right people. While such students may, upon graduation, feel satisfied with what the college has done for them, in terms of what the college could have done they have been woefully short-changed.

There are earnest young people who come with high hopes of realizing themselves, and of participating actively in a community of scholars.

Often they complain of limitations in the college situation which seem to thwart their hopes. But if these students persist in their own goals, the college experience may not disappoint them.

The worth of your own experience will depend upon the extent that you can relate yourself and your goals to the best that your college has to offer.

Education is essentially an *inner* experience, a personal growth. Many changes which take place during the college years are intangible and immeasurable; one can not relate just when and how they took place. One can not detect the exact point at which an insight into literature was achieved, or an appreciation of music, or an understanding of political action. These are essentially personal experiences: while the initial impact may have been slight, their consequences may last a lifetime.

Some effects of college are tangible and measurable. Such results can be most easily demonstrated from that part of one's education which is vocational or technical.

Only recently have educators studied the less easily discernible effects of college upon the students (1). A few studies have been made on the changes which occur during college. To an even more limited extent,

> *Education is that which remains when one has forgotten everything he learned in school.*
>
> —Albert Einstein

there have been studies which analyze the characteristics of college alumni. For example, one of the major "intangibles" which should result from your college education is the change that takes place in you, your own development as an educated person. This does not relate so much to your accumulation of knowledge as it does to your widened sympathies, new interests and desires, cultivated tastes, and heightened intellectual curiosity.

CHANGES OCCURRING DURING COLLEGE YEARS

The entering freshman.

Students entering American colleges show an extremely wide diversity of abilities, motivations, and interests. Although students in one college may differ considerably from those in another, there are also wide differences within any single college (2). One change which seems to occur during the college years is a trend toward reducing the diversity found originally among freshman.

Changes in knowledge and skills.

Of all the changes which may occur during the college years, the most clearly established are the increases in knowledge: When freshman scores on achievement tests are compared with the scores of sophomores, juniors, and seniors, it is clear that the college does succeed in transmitting significant amounts of knowledge. Similar results are found whether the different classes are compared with each other at the same time, or whether individual students are tested at various times during their college careers (3).

On the question of whether students in college actually develop the ability to think critically, an elaborate research study failed to produce a simple answer. It appears that students in social science did show gains in this ability over the period of years, but there were wide differences between colleges (4). Further research in this field seems to be required.

Changes in mental ability.

For many years psychologists believed that there could be little increase in the mental ability of a college student. By the time he entered college, his abilities were regarded as relatively stable. In recent years, however, this viewpoint has been questioned by many psychologists (5), and according to at least one study, the mental ability of a person can continue to increase even after middle age. In any event, it appears that few students are now making the maximum use of whatever potential they have and that learning can continue to take place throughout life.

Changes in attitudes and values.

Some extremely interesting research has been done on the extent of changes in student attitudes and values which occur during the college years (6). Dr. Phillip Jacob concludes that students show a greater homogeneity and consistency of values at the end of four years than when they began college (7). Studies of the values which students actually held during the 1950's clearly show an "inclination to seek a rich, full life for one's self and one's family; to think in concrete and practical terms about the material benefits—job, home, facilities for recreation

—that one expects to attain and enjoy." But at the same time they remained unconcerned about important social problems (8). In contrast, college students in other countries either stressed making a contribution to their country or stressed the building of their own characters and personalities.

In the early 1960's it seemed that more students were intellectually serious—they searched for greater breadth and unity of knowledge. They sought worthwhile commitments outside college. The majority of students, however, still regarded such matters as secondary to their concern for their own careers. By the late 1960's significant minorities were committed to changing the campus society and the world.

STUDIES OF ALUMNI

There are comparatively few studies of the characteristics of college alumni; even rarer are studies which compare them with individuals who have not completed college. As might be expected, there is more data on such relatively accessible matters as income and occupation than there is on beliefs, attitudes, and personality changes.

Income.

In the past there was evidence of a direct relationship between the amount of schooling and the amount of income, although it is not clear that a cause-and-effect relationship existed. Perhaps the drive and determination that enabled a student to survive the college years constituted the very factors enabling him to earn more income.

As more and more students complete college, the financial value of a college degree will tend to decrease. Moreover, the gap between the earnings of college-educated persons and others has tended to become narrower as a result of various social forces in this country.

Marriage and children.

College graduates at one time differed significantly from the rest of the population in certain characteristics. Fewer married; those who did married later and had fewer children. In recent years, these differences have become less evident as more students marry and have children at a younger age, sometimes while they are still attending college. One important distinction which still exists is that college graduates tend to marry other college graduates. They also tend to have a lower divorce rate than the rest of the population (9) and to be better parents.

Interests and values.

According to a number of studies, interests and values which students have while attending college are likely to be retained for a long time after graduation (10). William James felt "that outside of their own business, the ideas gained by men before they are twenty-five are practically the only ideas they shall have in their lives." There is some supporting evidence that college students show little change in their attitudes and opinions once they leave school.

Studies of college alumni show that graduates are not significantly different from the rest of the population in such cultural matters as the books or magazines they read and the music they listen to (11). There is some evidence that college graduates as a group are somewhat more conservative politically than the rest of the population (12).

According to one study, virtually every college graduate would choose to go to college again if he had his life to live over. Moreover, in most cases, he would return to the same college. Many graduates, however, were dissatisfied with the type of curriculum they had followed: about a third wished they had more specific training, and about a fifth wished for more general education (13).

WHAT COLLEGE CANNOT DO FOR YOU

Although the majority of college graduates report that they were generally satisfied with their college experience, some students and some graduates are not satisfied. In many cases this dissatisfaction is due to an exaggerated idea of what it is possible for a college to accomplish. Recently, a number of college deans and a number of students in twenty-five colleges and universities were asked to state what they thought a college could *not* do for its students. Surprisingly enough, there was general agreement among the respondents.

They said that a college could not be counted upon to create interest or excitement for learning. Thus, one dean of students said:

> There are [some] who enter expecting to be motivated and challenged by the experience of the faculty. These students have a fairly good perspective on themselves and wish to develop it. Yet they do not see themselves as basically responsible for excitement for learning or challenge of investigation. The burden of making education relevant does not rest with them since they are to some degree satisfied with the current operation of their intelligence.

And one average student wrote to me:

I don't believe a college can interest a student. The student must be interested in the school.

An honor student said:

College cannot do anything for a student who does not want to strive for the things which college can give one. If the student does not love books or have the desire for truth, it will only mean a worthless degree.

Several respondents repeated that a college could not be expected to make good students out of poor ones. One dean wrote:

I believe it's important for high school seniors to realize that college will be primarily an intellectual experience—that's the main reason for going, or should be. And in most instances they are not going to get by unless they have the necessary academic equipment. It is then essential for students to be realistic in their appraisals of themselves and in choosing colleges within the realm of their own scholastic ability.

Another dean said:

Far too many youngsters have ambitions which exceed their ability. I think a student must be realistic in his choices and must be aware that we have no panacea for a student who has performed poorly in the past.

Several writers stressed that college could not be expected to give easy answers to really important questions nor could it be relied upon to make major decisions for the individual. Of this an average student said:

A college does not make decisions for the student. It can present different things to the individual, but it is up to that person alone to choose. A college does nothing directly or materially for a person. It only shows the student how to do things for himself.

A college dean expressed it this way:

Many students first come to college with a greater degree of concern than is necessary about their life goals, academic interests, vocational choice. Often, they are overly anxious in this regard. Many expect the answers to these problems to come quickly, or easily. Unfortunately, the colleges can not solve the problems with a magic formula. There is usually no simple solution. It often takes time and students should learn to be patient. They should also avail themselves of the opportunity to take different types of courses in college to test their interests. They should talk with professors and fellow students to broaden their knowledge and profit from this information. They should seek professional counseling and testing, if available, to reaffirm their interests and to point out their strengths and limitations. They should not expect too much at first.

One student complained:

College cannot help me get the presents that I asked Santa Claus to give me. It can't prevent tooth decay or help build strong bodies 12 ways. Unfortunately it also only helps you in social intercourse, not sexual.

According to one writer, college cannot even be depended upon to inculcate intellectual tolerance:

College cannot teach a student to respect the other person's point of view. Colleges can perhaps foster an atmosphere wherein all points of view can be heard but in the end each person must develop his own appreciation and tolerance and understanding of others.

Finally, it should be borne in mind that college cannot be expected to complete the education of the individual. A lifetime is apparently not sufficient.

Many correspondents stressed how little the college could do to improve emotional maturity. They said it could not make students realistic, or happy, or mature and responsible. They could not create a value system for the individual, make him discipline himself, or give him any assistance at all unless he sought it. One junior college student wrote:

College can't make [the student] accept responsibility for himself. If a student doesn't have what it takes to plug in there and study, read and prepare for class, he won't learn.

A college dean expressed his thoughts somewhat differently:

For some it seems that they expect to enter and somehow or other at the end of four years be graduated as a completed and almost perfect product, problems solved, ready to be successful. There is little awareness of the work involved in mastering and assimilating subject matter, so that they will have the opportunity to live as intelligent, not just smart people. There seems to be little patience with the growing process measured in terms of responsibility acceptance. For those students disappointment comes early; and most often the blame is placed on the "system."

"College," remarked some of the writers, "cannot make students either popular or successful." As one student wrote:

It cannot provide a full social life. A college is a higher institution of learning, not a playground.

Another said:

College cannot make a success out of a loafer; it cannot make a stupid person smart. College life can only shape and mold slightly; it cannot change somebody completely.

In summary, the students and the administrators who responded to the survey agreed that there was virtually nothing the college could do to make changes in the student unless the student participated in the process. One important element in the student's ability to benefit from his college experience is the quality of preparation which he had before he came. In the next chapter, you will be able to compare your own preparation with that of other students.

NOTES TO CHAPTER 2

(1) See Mervin B. Freedman, *Impact of College* (New Dimensions in Higher Education, No. 4 [Washington, D.C.: U.S. Department of Health, Education, and Welfare, 1960]); Nevitt Sanford, *The American College*, chap. XXV.

(2) Paul Heist and Harold Webster—*Implications for Selection and Study of Undergraduates* (Berkeley, California: Center for the Study of Higher Education) (mimeographed), and John L. Holland, "Determinants of College Choice" (Evanston, Illinois: National Merit Scholarship Corporation) (mimeographed).

(3) C. R. Pace and G. G. Stern, "An Approach to the Measurement of Psychological Characteristics of College Environments," *Journal of Educational Psychology*, XLIX (1958), pp. 269-277.

(4) Paul L. Dressel and Lewis B. Mayhew, *General Education—Explorations in Evaluation* (Washington, D.C.: American Council on Education, 1954).

(5) Mervin B. Freedman, *Impact of College*, p. 9.

(6) See David Riesman, "Review of *Changing Values in College* by Phillip E. Jacob," in *American Sociological Review*, XXIII (1958), pp. 732, 738; J. M. Gillespie and G. W. Allport, *Youth's Outlook on the Future* (Garden City, New York: Doubleday and Co., Inc., 1955).

(7) Phillip E. Jacob, *Changing Values in College* (New York: Harper and Row, 1958).

(8) *Ibid.*; see also Edward D. Eddy, Jr., *The College Influence on Student Character* (Washington, D.C.: American Council on Education, 1959); Max Wise, *They Come for the Best of Reasons* (Washington, D.C.: American Council on Education, 1958); S. E. Harris (ed.), *Higher Education in the United States* (Cambridge, Mass.: Harvard University Press, 1960).

(9) P. C. Glick and Carter H. Glick, "Marriage Patterns and Educational Level," *American Sociological Review*, XXIII (1958), pp. 294-300; see also R. Shosteck, *Five Thousand Women College Graduates* (Washington, D. C.: B'nai B'rith Vocational Service, 1953).

(10) E. I. Kelly, "Consistency of the Adult Personality," *American Psychologist*, X (1955), pp. 659-681.
See also E. K. Strong, *Vocational Interests Eighteen Years After College* (Minneaplois, Minnesota: University of Minnesota Press, 1955).

(11) See C. Robert Pace, *They Went to College* (Minneapolis, Minnesota: University of Minnesota Press, 1941); C. Robert Pace, *Time Magazine Survey*, 1947.

(12) Phillip E. Jacob, *Changing Values in College*.

(13) Ernest Havemann and Patricia Salter West, *They Went to College*.

SUGGESTIONS FOR FURTHER READING

Barzun, Jacques, *The House of Intellect*, New York: Harper and Row, 1959 (Torch TB/1051).

Eddy, Edward D., Jr., *The College Influence on Student Character*, Washington, D. C.: American Council on Education, 1959.

Gillespie, J. M. and Allport, G. W., *Youth's Outlook on the Future*. Garden City, New York: Doubleday and Co., Inc., 1955.

Jacob, Phillip E., *Changing Values in College*. New York: Harper and Row, 1958.

Whyte, William H., Jr., *The Organization Man*. New York: Simon and Schuster, 1957 (Anchor Books A 117).

Wise, Max, *They Come for the Best of Reasons*. Washington, D. C.: American Council on Education, 1958.

VIEWPOINT

The Freshman Myth
BY GEORGE G. STERN

Do freshman expect too much of college?
Where do they get these ideas?
How do some students react to disillusionment?
What does the author suggest as a solution?

No matter what sort of college they are entering, college freshmen of the sixties appear to share a misconception as to what they will find on the campus. Regardless of whether the new alma mater is a big university or a small college, freshmen arriving there expect more of it than any one institution is prepared to provide.

When 3,075 new freshmen at four universities and colleges filled out a questionnaire (the *College Characteristics Index*) on the basis of what they expected of their college, most of them at each school showed themselves to be under the influence of the same unrealistic expectations. Though they were enrolling at institutions as different from each other in location, philosophy, and goals as St. Louis, Beloit, Cazenovia Junior College, and Syracuse, only a Utopia U. could have lived up to their expectations.

The items on the CCI questionnaire refer to eleven factors, curricular and extracurricular, related to all aspects of college life. Freshmen in the study expected their particular school to have more to offer in almost every aspect of college activity than one college in six actually provides in even one aspect.

The young hopefuls visualized that their schools would have extensive extracurricular programs—as elaborate as those found in certain denominational schools—and their expectations regarding academic opportunities would have been fulfilled only at one of the small number of highly selective elite liberal arts colleges.

The students revealed that they were poorly informed about the composite character of their individual college. They showed no realization of the fact that schools which maximize the intellectual climate minimize provisions for extracurricular activities. These freshmen expected their schools to do as much for their social life as for their intellectual growth.

Students' expectations were most realistic with regard to the amount of student autonomy their college would allow, the degree of freedom they expected to

Dr. Stern, professor of psychology, Syracuse (New York) University, discussed this topic at greater length at the National Conference of the Association for Higher Education, 1966. This article was reported in the N.E.A. Journal, (September 1966), Vol. LV, No. 6, pp. 41-43. By permission.

find being about what actually exists on the whole across the country—less than is to be found at many good independent liberal arts colleges, but more than the typical large university.

On the other hand, freshmen were way off with regard to the emphasis the colleges place on self-expression. They singled out in particular those activities that involve the development of social commitment and political individuality. More than three-fourths of these incoming classes believed that their school expected them to "develop a strong sense of responsibility about their role in contemporary social and political life," and that this would not only involve "developing ideals but also expressing them in action."

They thought that their fellow students and the faculty were going to be "actively concerned about national and international affairs," that a "number of prominent professors play a significant role in national or local politics," and that students would be "encouraged to take an active part in social reforms and political programs."

An even higher percentage of the freshmen believed that "no one needs to be afraid of expressing extreme or unpopular view points in this school," since "it has an excellent reputation for academic freedom" and "the values most stressed here are open-mindedness and objectivity."

Where do the entering freshmen get their boundless enthusiasm, their idealistic expectations about college? What is the source of the myths so many of them believe?

It's certainly not generated by the common needs of the freshmen themselves. Personality data for students in the study indicate that they are a relatively heterogeneous group. Unlike the small minority of liberal nonconformists who are entering elite liberal arts colleges, they reveal no tendencies as a group toward political activism or even high academic motivation. What they expect of the colleges is what they believe is supposed to be going on in higher education.

Upperclassmen or faculty members are not responsible for the freshmen's never-never land concept of college life. Response of *these* groups to the CCI questionnaire show that they are aware of the striking and distinctive characteristics of their own schools as compared with others.

The freshmen themselves tell us that they formulate their ideas about what college will be like on the basis of information they get from friends, family, and high school counselors. Possibly all three of these groups have an inaccurate impression of what college is like.

Analysis of faculty and second year students' CCI responses at one of the colleges in this study revealed an academic environment that is relatively depressing and a far cry from freshmen expectations, whereas trustees came up with some unique impressions of their own.

In this school, only one group—the administrators—shared the freshman myth, and this fact may be a clue to the origin of the freshman myth. Administration, counselors, parents, and freshmen all read the college catalog, a publication that is generally about as sincere as a seed catalog.

Another possible source of the myth may be that teachers and parents (by way of dangling a carrot in front of the donkey's nose) knowingly present the collegian with an idealized picture of college life. To make the academic life more appealing, they invest it with the promise of greater demands (and therefore worth striving for) and greater rewards.

Whatever its source, the freshman myth may be responsible for some of today's campus unrest. The student arrives with such great expectations that he is almost certain to be disillusioned by what really happens on the campus. The disillusionment is nowhere greater than on the campuses of the big universities, and these institutions have been particularly vulnerable to student demonstrations.

Size alone is not the critical variable, however. Even schools like Brandeis, Drew, and Lafayette, with enrollments under 2,000, have had confrontations with their students in the last few years.

The disillusionment and dissatisfaction of an idealistic student body led by a militant minority of students and faculty eager to achieve institutional reforms has, in fact, resulted in student rebellions in other times, as well. The six rebellions at Princeton between 1800 and 1830 and the one at Harvard in 1823 that resulted in the expulsion of over half the graduating class were similar in ideologic background to the uprisings of today's students.

The issues in those days involved the lingering forms of puritanism; the problem now is the final overcoming of paternalism. The press for equality and democratization that de Tocqueville saw as the central genius of American culture has now reached the last and largest of the remaining underprivileged minorities, the young adults.

Today's students, loath to abandon their illusions when confronted with reality, are exerting great pressure to make their colleges become so many Utopia U's. If heeded, their demands for joint participation in curriculum changes, for innovations such as the teach-in and the new faculty-student administrative committees, and for the elimination of the use of grades as a coercive device would result in a college community in which academic strength would combine with personal intimacy, a model which has no earlier prototype in American higher education.

CHAPTER 3

Are Freshmen Prepared for College?

Freshmen tend to think that coming to college means that a completely new life is opening for them. They soon find that many problems they face have a peculiar and unexpected familiarity. Still tied firmly to their past, they are forced to confront new situations armed mainly with whatever habits and skills they have brought with them.

There are, of course, many differences between going to high school and going to college, but the similarities are greater than most students anticipate. The freshman still has the values and attitudes which he has developed over the years. He has acquired a repertory of study habits and a history of academic success or disappointment. His parents still remain a great influence upon him, whether he accepts or rejects their values. In addition, every student comes with a socio-economic background that strongly affects his adjustment to college, just as it has influenced his adjustment to high school.

The purpose of this chapter is to help the freshman to understand his present situation by examining the influences that have affected him in the past. Such a review undoubtedly will reveal both strengths and weaknesses in the student's background. However, our purpose here is not to blame and not to commend, but rather to understand. Now, it may be asked whether it does any good for a student already in college to discuss the preparation he had before he came. There are many reasons why this discussion may be useful for him. For example, deficiencies in his preparation may be the main cause for difficulties he may now be having. On the other hand, his preparation might be found adequate and the cause of his problems might be elsewhere. Obviously, such different cases require different remedies. It is even possible that careful examination of the student's past may help him decide whether he is actually in the college where he has the greatest chance to succeed.

For most students one of the main values of college is an increase in understanding of themselves and of their own potential. "Study the past," said Confucius, "if you would divine the future."

> *Colleges become storehouses of knowledge because freshmen bring so much in, and seniors take so little out.*
> Attributed to Charles W. Eliot

INFLUENCES AFFECTING SUCCESS IN COLLEGE

Parental influences affect students.

In most cases, a student attends college with the active help and encouragement of his parents. They believe that college is worthwhile for their child and are willing to support him in college, even to the extent of making considerable financial sacrifices. Typically, they also took an interest in his high school studies and helped him to prepare for college. They realize that education means change, and they are prepared to accept new ideas. In such instances, the student may derive strength from the knowledge that his parents respect him and have confidence in him (1). Secure in this knowledge, he is able to make realistic plans and is able to work more efficiently after entering college. There are, of course, cases where the attitude of the parents seems to be encouraging, yet the student, in his desire for independence, rebels against them and rejects any advice they may offer.

39

In other instances the attitude of parents is directly harmful to the student's chance of success in college. Certain parents, despite their love for their children, are overcritical toward them. They begin by excessively supervising their child's elementary and high school preparation. They drive him to study, curtail his privileges, harass him incessantly, and altogether make study so unpleasant that he may rebel and refuse to do his best. A student from such a background may develop insecurity and frustration which interfere with his studies. When parents set unrealistic standards, the children not only fail to reach these standards but, as a result of failure, may be prevented from realizing their own potential abilities.

Parents often cannot face the fact that their child may lack the intellectual ability and the personal motivation to succeed in a particular college. They know the career the child should follow and they know he will succeed; they cannot be swayed. They disregard their child's record in high school and have no faith in any psychological tests. They believe that if their child is only given a chance to attend college, somehow a miracle will come to pass: In a short time the college will be able to produce a completely different individual, but one who will turn out to be exactly what his parents had always wanted, successful, polished, professional, yet essentially unchanged. In short, they want their children to learn from the greatest minds of all time, but to arrive at the same conclusions the parents have always held.

In contrast, there are parents whom psychologists label over-protective—those who try to protect their young from the consequences of their acts, making excuses for failure by blaming it on schools, teachers, "evil companions," and everything but their children's own inadequacies.

There are also parents who are completely indifferent toward their children's preparation for college, and some who actively discourage their children from attending. Parents may regard college as a waste of time and money, or as a place where young people get strange ideas and get into trouble. To them, college may be a place for their son but certainly not for their daughter. Parental attitudes such as these are not helpful to the college student who needs all the help he can get.

Finally, there is a growing number of parents who are frankly baffled by their children and by the entire college process. They launch their sons and daughters into an uncertain sea and hope for the best.

Community and social class affect college preparation.

American high schools tend to reflect the values of widely differing local communities as well as the differences which exist among the various social classes (2). In some communities every high school student is expected to go to college. Such a college-oriented community actively supports its high school and takes a great interest in the students' progress. Curriculum, activities, and counseling are all geared toward college preparation. A college freshman who attended such a high school obviously has an advantage over a freshman who attended a different kind of high school.

In contrast, high schools in some communities do not expect most of their students to continue studying. College education may be regarded as a desirable but unattainable goal. Nevertheless, the school does offer some college preparatory courses along with terminal vocational programs. These high schools are usually found in communities of lower socioeconomic status. Their graduates may enter college with a definite handicap despite the fact that their potential ability may be equal or superior to that of the graduates from the college-oriented community (3).

Numerous studies have confirmed that social classes with their own characteristic values and attitudes are an established part of American life (4). The social class to which a person belongs is not entirely a matter of income. A truck driver may make more money than a high school teacher, yet the driver derives less social status and prestige from his occupation. Although the American class structure is not rigid, it still has a great influence in determining who goes to college and how well he adjusts once he arrives there.

In the past, members of the so-called lower or culturally deprived classes were not very interested in college. Recently, however, more children from such backgrounds have begun to attend. Since college is traditionally a middle-class institution, stressing such middle-class values as social conformity and postponed benefits, the student from a lower-class home often has the special problem of adjusting to new social-class expectations and, at the same time, coming to terms with his former values and attitudes. Moving from one social class to another is never an easy process.

Many lower-class parents look upon college as the primary means by which their own children may achieve upward mobility. The lower-class young people themselves hold this attitude to a somewhat lesser extent but still, between 40 and 50 per cent of them believe in the need for a college education (5). Professor Frank Reissman of Bard College has pointed out several factors which inhibit a culturally deprived person from entering college, even though he may desire to do so. First, he believes that further education is out of his reach. Second, he is often unfamiliar with the mechanics of entering a college. Third, most of his friends and relatives have not attended college and he is afraid he will be out of place. Finally, he is afraid that he will break his old ties with his family and friends (6).

Middle-class parents look forward to having their children attend college. They expect the college to furnish vocational preparation, cultural development, and an opportunity to be with the "right people." Their children, already familiar with middle-class values, may find it easy to adjust to college socially. Some of these students, however, may go through a period of conscious rebellion against the values of their parents. Unfortunately, rebellion can be as restricting as conformity.

For better or worse, adjustment to college is often influenced by social class.

Nonintellectual factors affect achievement.

Students are often surprised to find that success in college is dependent upon nonintellectual factors as well as upon intelligence. During high school, grades and academic performance were what mattered, while emotional and social factors were often less important. During college these factors can become so overwhelming that students with excellent high school records sometimes fail to graduate from college.

Some students operate with great energy, accepting the obligations of college classes as a part of the learning process. Such a student may have occasional doubts about his abilities and at times may even be anxious because of the fear of failure, but he is able to control and direct his fears and anxieties.

Other students, however, with equal potential academic ability are less able to control or direct their fears and anxieties. Terror-stricken, they are unable to cope with their problems.

Some students yield readily to the patterns of the peer group, while others do not. Students differ in confidence, concentration, and in classroom effectiveness. Intellectual ability and potential cannot account for such differences in behavior.

Academic preparation affects students.

Many students complain that they are faced with academic disappointments at college.

When I see what I'm expected to know, I wonder what I did in four years of high school. I now find I don't know even how to read or write.

They give us these long reading assignments and I spend all evening doing just one chapter.

Every day in class I find them mentioning people I've never heard of and I'm expected to know them. Where I come from nobody knows Oedipus from T. S. Eliot.

I know that it didn't do much good in high school to tell me to study harder, but I wish now that someone could have *convinced* me that this was necessary. I expected college to be difficult, but not anywhere as difficult as it really turns out to be. It is a good deal like high school as far as class work is concerned except that it is twice as intensive, and goes about twice as fast.

At one time, preparation for college had a specific meaning in the United States. High school students were required to take rigorous college preparatory classes and there was great stress on English rhetoric and mathematics. Their goals were usually well defined and the students had a fairly clear idea of what they would find in college. In contrast, today's high school graduate may have had little specific preparation for college. His decision to attend may have been reached without either serious thought or a realistic appraisal of his own assets and liabilities. Consequently, students differ widely in their academic preparation for college. Often they have not read the books the college assumes they have, nor have they acquired even the most basic and indispensable skills of reading and writing.

College students are usually expected to find their own answers, while high school students generally expect the teacher to furnish the answers. This constitutes one major academic difference between some colleges and some high schools. In colleges where there is stress on individual research, students may find themselves at a loss if they have had no previous experience of this kind. They may regard the instructor as not interested in them simply because he does not provide them with answers, or always tell them how to find the answers for themselves. Students may be particularly upset and confused when they bring in what they regard as final answers only to find that the instructor raises still more questions.

There seems to be little relationship between the specific courses a student took in high school and the grades he receives in the liberal arts college, although, according to research, students who have received the better grades in high school English do better in the college liberal arts program (7). Taking a particular set of courses in high school does not of itself guarantee success in college. What is more important is the general level of the high school performance. The entering freshman, therefore, need not be overly discouraged if he missed taking certain courses in high school.

Financial factors may affect success in college.

Several studies show that high school graduates who had part-time jobs may do as well or better in college than their classmates who did not work. On the other hand, there certainly are high school students whose college preparation suffers because they have to divert time and energy to earning their way.

Although lack of finances is often given as the reason for leaving college, several studies tend to indicate that frequently this lack is not the real reason; it is given as a convenient but superficial explanation (8).

EVALUATING YOUR PREPARATION

For success in college, a student must make a new and realistic appraisal of his own background and potential including the results of his aptitude tests. Chapter 14 discusses in detail some ways of making this appraisal, but a few preliminary comments may be in order here.

No matter what attitudes the student may have had while he was in high school, he is forced to reappraise himself when entering college. He may find that the goals he formerly cherished are no longer meaningful. Other goals and values have come forward to take their places.

In short, every student must ask himself what he wants and whether it is worth wanting. He must then ask what the possibilities are for accomplishing his purpose. Then, he must take action. George Bernard Shaw said:

> **People are always blaming their circumstances for what they are. I don't believe in circumstances. The people who get on in this world are the people who get up and look for the circumstances they want, and if they don't find them, make them.**

Some students in college discover they have abilities and talents which were never suspected:

> **I actually enjoy solving my own problems. I never had a chance to do this before I came. I've been traveling down a one-way street which has been going anywhere but where I want to go. For once I'm taking a hard look at myself.**

Other students may suddenly find themselves beyond their depth in college, even though they did very well in high school. A talent which was greatly admired back home may be considered quite ordinary at the state university.

> **I was a top student in my high school class and now they put me in remedial English . . . Why can't I get any recognition at college? Everyone used to make a fuss about my poetry, and it was even printed in our local weekly newspaper.**

Making use of tests.

Ordinarily a freshman has the results of a number of psychological tests available, and these can be of great help in his evaluation. But their limitations as well as their possibilities must be understood.

Test scores are only good estimates; they are not precise measures. A student may believe erroneously that a score of 120 makes him superior to a student receiving a score of 118. This is not necessarily so. Results vary from test to test and from time to time, and no single test can predict human behavior accurately. Tests can not tell a student whether he will succeed in a particular occupation, nor can they make decisions for him. A student often believes that his high score on an interest test guarantees his success in some specific occupation. Unfortunately, this is not true.

In the area of intelligence testing, psychologists believe that no direct measure of potential mental ability has ever been devised. All that they can do is to infer mental ability from what is basically an achievement test. Mental ability tests thus are not the last word on academic success, for they do not measure such important factors as motivations, drives, and study skills, all of which are closely related to success in college.

Experience has shown that certain combinations of test scores do distinguish between students accurately enough to make the test useful. Many students make the mistake of taking test results too lightly, particularly when their results are low. Such students may believe that hard work and high motivation can make a college graduate out of almost anyone, but students who score very low on the standard tests usually have difficulty in completing their freshman year.

In the next chapter, there will be a discussion of academic problems as well as many of the other problems that freshmen face.

NOTES TO CHAPTER 3

(1) Nevitt Sanford found that at Vassar the most important factor distinguishing good students from poor ones was that the mothers of the good students had intellectual interests or aspirations, and their fathers did not disapprove of intellectual women. The poorest students were those whose mothers had urged college purely for social prestige, and whose fathers were either dubious or contemptuous of higher education for girls. *Ladies Home Journal* (May, 1957), p. 198.

(2) James Bryant Conant, *Slums and Suburbs* (New York: McGraw-Hill Book Co. 1961), pp. 80-109.

(3) *Ibid.*

John Finley Scott in his "So You're Going to College!" (*Public Affairs Pamphlet*) points to a questionnaire distributed to college freshmen which asked: "Who gave you what turned out to be the *worst* advice about going to college?" About two-thirds named their high school counselor as being ill-informed about what their colleges required.

(4) See W. Lloyd Warner, Marchia Meeker, and Kenneth Eells, *Social Class in America* (New York: Harper & Row, 1960).

(5) Frank Riessman, *The Culturally Deprived Child* (New York: Harper & Row, 1962), p. 11.

(6) *Ibid.*, p. 14

(7) David R. Cook and William O. Martinson, "Relationship of Certain Course Work in High School to Achievement in College," *Personnel and Guidance Journal*, XL (1962), pp. 703-707.

(8) R. E. Iffert, *Retention and Withdrawal of College Students* (Washington, D. C.: U.S. Government Printing Office, 1958).

SUGGESTIONS FOR FURTHER READING

Brownstein, S. C. and M. Weiner, *You Can Win A Scholarship*. New York: Barron's Educational Series, Inc., 1964.

Feingold, S. N., *Latest Information on Scholarships in the Space Age.* Cambridge, Mass.: Bellman and Company, 1965.

Fine, Benjamin and S. A. Eisenberg, *How to Get Money for College*. New York: Doubleday and Co., Inc., 1964.

Governmental Publications

Division of Student Financial Aid, Office of Education, U. S. Department of Health, Education and Welfare, Washington, D.C. 20202. (Write for information regarding loans under the National Defense Educational Act.)
Bureau of State Services, U. S. Department of Health, Education and Welfare, Washington, D.C. 20201. (Write for information regarding loans under the Health Profession Education Assistance Act for students interested in becoming physicians, dentists, osteopaths, and optometrists. Information regarding loans under the Nursing Student Loan Program may also be obtained.)
Public Inquiry Branch, U. S. Department of Health, Education, and Welfare, Washington, D.C. 20201. (Write for information regarding scholarships for students training to be teachers.)

Kessler, O. P., *A National Catalog of Scholarships and Other Financial Aids for Students Entering College*. Dubuque, Iowa: W. C. Brown Company, 1963.

Lovejoy, C. E. and T. S. Jones, *Lovejoy-Jones College Scholarship Guide* (rev. ed.). New York: Simon and Schuster, 1968.

Lovejoy, C. E., *College Guide* (8th ed.). New York: Simon and Schuster, 1966.

McKee, Richard, *Financial Assistance for College Students*. (Write to Superintendent of Documents, Washington, D. C. 20402).

New York Life Insurance Company, *The Cost of a College Education*. New York. (Write to the company for the latest issue.)

Prudential Insurance Company of America, *Facing Facts About College Costs*. Newark, New Jersey, 1964.

Smith, G. Kerry, *Stress and Campus Response*, San Francisco: Jossey-Bass Inc., 1968.

Splaver, Sarah. *Your College Education—How to Pay for It*. New York: Jules Messner, Inc., 1964.

VIEWPOINT

Who Should Go to College?

BY JOHN DALE RUSSELL

*What are the two major approaches to the question of who
should go to college?*
*Who should be responsible for determining whether or not
a particular individual should be admitted?*
*How important are high school grades from the viewpoint
of some college admissions officers?*
What keeps potentially capable students out of college?

College attendance in the United States is rapidly becoming democratized. It
is no longer the privilege of the few. . . .

This spectacular expansion has raised a question about the desirability of
offering college opportunities to so many young people.

° ° °

Two somewhat different answers are currently given to the question, "Who
should go to college?"

One answer: In a democratic society all who wish to continue their education
and who have the ability to pursue college-level studies should be provided
opportunity.

The other answer: Only as many should be educated as are necessary to
supply the demand in occupations requiring college-level preparation.

Extend Opportunity?

The necessity for educating all youth to the highest levels they are capable
of reaching and eager to attain is frequently justified. This line of argument
holds that education in a democracy is a right to which each person is entitled.
Proper education of the individual is necessary for his effective development,
in order that he may compete on equal terms with others of similar talents and
enjoy fully the privileges of living in a democracy.

From this point of view the duty of society is to provide every young person
opportunity to continue his education to the highest level he is capable of
attaining.

A second line of argument supporting a broad opportunity for education
holds that this is one of the greatest factors in national welfare and security.

An enlightened citizenry is essential to the success of the democratic form
of government. The extent of our material wealth and the wide availability

Dr. Russell is professor emeritus at New York University. This article first appeared in
the *Journal of the National Education Association*, XXXVII, No. 7 (1948), 448-9, and is
reprinted by permission.

of the comforts of life depend closely on the number of well educated persons who are equipped to operate the machinery of economic production.

The relations of a person within his family, community, state, nation, and the world can be maintained on a satisfactory basis today only by appropriate and extensive education.

The surest protection against radical and revolutionary change lies in the education of all our citizens. At the same time, the greatest assurance of orderly, evolutionary progress toward a better society rests on a wide distribution of education.

The argument on the basis of the welfare of the social order would lay a responsibility on society for educating *all* to the limits of their capability, without much regard for the individual's willingness to sacrifice to obtain the education. Completion of his education becomes as much a duty of the citizen as bearing arms in time of war.

Perhaps education at the higher levels cannot be forced on an individual in the same manner as military service.

It is however, at least the duty of society to see that its capable young people are counseled suitably and its educational program organized attractively at the higher levels, so as to induce the largest possible number to complete all the education they are capable of attaining.

Limit Opportunity?

But there is the other answer to "Who should go to college?" which would limit that opportunity in terms of the jobs available to people with college preparation.

Some observers have been fearful that an overextension of educational opportunities would produce more doctors, lawyers, ministers, school teachers, engineers, and others professionally prepared than can find employment.

o   o   o

In the first place, much of the extended education should be of a general sort, not occupational, but for citizenship and cultural purposes. This kind of education can never be overproduced in a democratic society.

In the second place, demand for persons in occupations requiring college preparation seems to be increasing as rapidly as enrolments.

o   o   o

The two answers to the question, "Who should go to college?" may thus be reconciled: *All who have the ability and incentive should go to college, but they should be given guidance so that they may distribute themselves suitably among various lines of occupational preparation.*

College Ability?

What is meant by "ability" to pursue college-level studies? Admittedly there are no fixed rules or objective measures by which one can unerringly distinguish in advance those young men and women capable of succeeding in college.

Indeed, certain time-honored requirements for admission have been shown by careful investigations not to be valid criteria. For example, no one subject of highschool study, such as Latin, seems to have any particular merit as preparation for college, when other factors affecting the success of the student, such as his intelligence, are taken into account.

General intellectual ability, as measured by a psychological test, affords a fairly good index of college ability, especially when used in combination with average grades in highschool or rank in highschool class. The best possible combination of such objective measures, however, yields a prediction of success in college that is only about 50 per cent better than a guess.

Personal motivation represents perhaps the largest area of unmeasured traits that need to be taken into account in advising students about attending college.

Who Should Decide?

Who should be responsible for determining whether or not a given individual should be admitted to college?

Traditionally, the colleges have assumed the right to select their own entering students. At every other stage in the educational system, however, teachers in the unit the pupil is completing customarily determine whether he is ready for the next rung of the educational ladder.

Chief exception to the rule that the college selects its own students is found in publicly controlled institutions of higher education, which now in many states admit any graduate of an accredited highschool.

Most institutions also have a policy of admitting mature persons, often defined as those over 21 years of age, as special students without regard to the specified entrance requirements.

These policies seem to be based on two ideas: (1) The highschool staff that has taught the student for four years knows more about his ability than the college can discover through entrance requirements and tests. (2) Motivation is so important a factor in academic success that every person who really wants to go to college should have the opportunity to try it. These assumptions seem sound, provided effective counsel and guidance are furnished.

°   °   °

Barriers Today

The present system of higher education in the United States, even with the recent expansions in enrolment, falls far short of the goal of providing every citizen all the education he is capable of attaining.

Among significant barriers now blocking achievement of this goal are: (1) cost of going to college; (2) shortage of facilities, both physical plant and teaching staff; (3) concentration of institutions in relatively few centers in each state; (4) unattractiveness of much of the instruction offered in colleges and universities and their frequent failure to offer programs that meet modern needs; (5) inadequacy of counseling and guidance services at all levels of the school system.

These barriers must be overcome before it can be said that all who should go to college are able to avail themselves of the opportunity.

VIEWPOINT

Is College Education Wasted on Women?

BY NEVITT SANFORD

Why do girls go to college?
Do they get very much out of it?
What is the greatest obstacle to a college education?
How much influence does a college have on its graduates twenty years later?
Is it unfeminine to be intelligent?

It is no news that there are and always have been women students who go through four years of college without being appreciably influenced by their academic work. Our research at Vassar has, I believe, thrown some new light on this problem. This research is, primarily, a study of how and why students change as they go through college. It has sought to find means by which college education might be made more effective. The difficulties, the problems, have come in for more attention than the successes and happy endings.

It is generally assumed in this country that the more education, the better. We have come to look on college in much the same way that we used to look on high school. Our kids will go if we can afford it and if they can get in. What else, indeed, are we to do with an 18-year-old girl who is not needed at home, and who is not yet ready for marriage? The inevitable result has been that thirst for knowledge does not rank very high among the motives that girls have for going to college.

o   o   o

College teachers recall, or imagine, the "good old days" prior to the First World War; the days when girls who went to college were a pretty special group, out to change the world. They were out to show what women could do; at the least, to prepare themselves for careers that required special training. Figures from the Bureau of Labor Statistics confirm our own observations that a smaller and smaller proportion of college girls today want to prepare themselves for professional work. The marriage age for college women moves steadily lower. In Vassar of 1904 the average age at the time of marriage was 29. This year's seniors, on the average, expect to be married by 23; the freshmen hope to be wives by 22.

Dr. Sanford is professor of psychology at the University of California. This article appeared in the *Ladies' Home Journal*, May 1957, 78-9, 198. Reprinted by permission.

Feminism is dead, and probably few will mourn its passing. But in the absence of the strong motive which it generated, and in a culture in which merely being intellectual does not cut much ice, it is difficult for girls to stick to high intellectual purposes.

Psychology and psychiatry have contributed their share to the notion that the best way for a girl to show that she is healthy, wholesome, mature, well-adjusted and the like is to get married and have children. We should not be surprised if many girls have drawn the conclusion that the sooner this is accomplished, the better. Many neglect their self-development in favor of what they suppose the young men want. In the list of imagined qualities, being intellectual or "brainy" does not rank very high.

The college of today, then, has its work cut out for it. The residential college in particular selects students carefully, and regards flunking them out as a misfortune for all concerned. It takes considerable responsibility for the motivations and all-round well-being of the students, as well as for their intellectual diet. Thus it tries hard to interest students, to show them the satisfactions of learning, to instill a system of values in which the free use of one's mind looms large.

Here the greatest obstacle, according to our observations, is what might be called the student culture. This is a pattern of values, attitudes, ideas, ways of looking at things, rules of conduct and the like which prevails among the students at a college at any particular time. It is shaped to some extent by what students bring with them from their homes and communities and by what is the going thing in our society at large. But this student culture has an existence of its own and is passed on from one student generation to the next. The major concern of the entering freshman is with acceptance by her fellow students; her high-road to acceptance is by fitting in with the prevailing culture.

The student culture that we have observed at Vassar may have some unique features, but we have good reason to believe it is similar to what may be found in most leading women's colleges today. Some of the major features of this culture are the following:

Toward one another students are expected to be friendly, co-operative, pleasant. Toward the faculty, polite, dutiful, impersonal. The college work is to be taken seriously, but not too seriously. Frivolity is discouraged; but outstanding scholarly work, though tolerated, is not applauded. The emphasis is on moderation, keeping everyone on the same level of behavior and accomplishment. If a student thinks too much or talks too much, if she is either too indifferent or too ambitious, the student culture has effective means for bringing her into line.

With respect to ideas and issues, the thing is to be open-minded and noncontroversial, above all to avoid unpleasantness. If an ethical decision has to be made, the proper course is to find out what others think.

• • •

One of the main functions of the student culture is to keep the faculty at a respectful distance. It serves as a shield to prevent any deep involvements with courses or ideas, or any adult relationship with faculty members that might threaten the girls' satisfaction with themselves as they are or with the views they already have.

At any given time, a majority of the girls are accepting the student culture and participating in it more or less fully. Only a small minority succeed in remaining entirely aloof. Those whose outlook is quite different from that of the majority tend to drop out of college in the first two years. This is not to say that academic work plays no part. Most students are interested, even enthusiastic, about at least some of their courses and academic achievements. Many freshmen worry a great deal about their ability to keep up, especially those who come directly from public high school. The student body in general are not indifferent to academic work or unaffected by it. But, except for a minority, the philosophy and aims of the college are not the major influences in the formation of values and habits of life.

For the greater number, the student culture is the prime educational force at work. They use it as a guidepost for getting along with fellow students; for their thinking about men, marriage, and the world in **general**; for dealing with the faculty in such a way as to withstand their influence, yet keep relations pleasant. It makes up the central core of values and attitudes to which the students' academic experiences are assimilated.

It will be clear, then, that the task of the faculty is a very difficult one. The materials they would mold are pretty resistant to begin with. The competing influences, that would mold the materials in a different way, are formidable. Yet there is no doubt that by the time they have completed four years at Vassar, students in general have changed in ways that the college desires. Our tests show that seniors, as compared with freshmen, have more knowledge of their cultural heritage and more highly cultivated tastes and interests. They have greater mental flexibility, greater capacity to suspend judgment until the facts are known, greater tolerance and understanding toward others. They have more insight into themselves, more awareness of inner life. They are more independent and non-conforming, more self-confident, more realistic. And so on.

But nobody claims that the college's batting average is high enough. For that matter, no one knows for sure just how much these changes are due to the college and how much to natural growth. And the fact remains that differences among seniors are large; some have made enormous gains of the sort just described; in others—a great many—the gains have been slight.

But now comes the dilemma for the girl with whom college has "taken." We find that many seniors are thrown into a state of confusion and anxiety. They must decide what they will do with their lives from now on. For many students it is the first important decision they have had to make. Since, for many, the idea has somehow become implanted that they must choose between marriage and serious work, they hesitate to commit themselves to a career. On the other hand, they suspect—not without foundation—that there is no real place in our society for the liberally educated person who is not identified with some accomplishment or activity. And they suspect that the values gained in college will be out of place in the social world they are about to enter. The conflict is likely to be strongest for more serious students, since those not deeply committed to a discipline can abandon it more readily. In fact, anticipation of this kind of conflict is a major reason why many students avoid serious commitment to any interest throughout their college career.

Many observers have commented on the "flight into marriage" that so often takes place at this time. Some of these marriages are very good ones. They are based on a long acquaintance, and the girls are ready for the demands of married life. Many seniors, however, rush into marriage, hardly knowing the man involved, as a way of resolving the dilemma thrust upon them by graduation. Our alumnae samplings indicate that marriages undertaken for this reason have not worked out very well.

The majority of those who do not marry immediately work at something well below the level of their ability. Or else they attend graduate school for one or a few years, as a way of marking time until the "right man" comes along.

Students with professional ambitions often fare best during the senior year. Although virtually all of them plan to marry, marriage is for them an activity in which they will voluntarily choose to participate rather than something that is necessary for any sense of personal identity. Such students have a clear sense of direction, a greater degree of independence and self-confidence than most.

But preparation for a professional career is not the primary aim of liberal education. It aims, rather, to train the individual so that she can be intelligent in whatever she does. Above all, it aims to develop the individual so that her sense of herself as a real person does not depend on her being in any particular social role, such as wife and mother or working woman. The expectation today is that almost all college girls will, at one time or another, be wives and mothers and work at something outside the home. The hope is that as wives and mothers they will maintain a high level of culture and have a keen sense of being alive and worthy; and that when they work, they will do something important and interesting. The evidence is that, in general, the abilities and qualities that make for success in one of these areas also make for success in the other.

College is crucial for the development of these abilities and qualities. If a girl feels that she is "not living" now when she is in college, the chances are she will feel the same way ten or twenty or thirty years from now. The notion that things will be different when her circumstances have changed, when she is married or when she is engaged in "interesting work," is probably an illusion. Boredom in college is associated with boredom later on. The student who is not enjoying the academic aspects of her college life right now is not just headed for trouble; she is already in trouble.

This is a major conclusion from our intensive study of a group of Vassar alumnae twenty to twenty-five years out of college. Close acquaintance with this group of women would be enough to renew anyone's faith in the aims and processes of liberal education. These were women who had improved everything they had touched, and they had touched a great deal. But we are here talking about problems and difficulties. Everybody knows about the problems, and the achievements, of the career woman who does not marry. What concerned us particularly was the type of woman whose children had more or less grown up and who, now that external demands on her were withdrawn, was hard put to it to escape a sense of emptiness and boredom. Her inclination was to fill her time either with trivial social activities or with some routine "job" which though essentially meaningless gave her a sense of being busy.

We were concerned because we believed we saw here the probable future of today's social-minded college girl. The women of whom I speak had entered college because it was the thing to do, immersed themselves in the student culture, treated their academic work as an imposed nuisance, assumed vaguely that as soon as they were married to a good provider everything would be rosy. The resemblance to the majority of today's students is too close for comfort.

Another conclusion from the study of alumnae: even those in whom education had taken well found it difficult to maintain the values and interests developed in college. Those who had kept up either had professional careers or had married men who shared or admired the college-bred outlook.

° ° °

. . . When the GI's were returning from the war and filling the colleges and graduate schools, young women had all sorts of imaginative designs for married living. Today, and in more recent years, their ideas are more traditional and conventional.

In the time of the Cold War the crisis has not been great enough to require that all hands pitch in and do useful work. But it has been great enough to place accent on the "manly virtues" in men and traditional virtues in women. Not only is feminism dead; we have passed into a phase of antifeminism. Clever writers berate women for exercising their new-found rights and privileges. Psychologists and psychiatrists issue grim warnings about mothers' responsibilities to their young children. Thus it is that we have an upsurge of the attitude that one must not appear too bright or too competent, lest this threaten one's ability to take traditional feminine roles.

It ought not to be necessary to say that if a woman is too assertive and bossy, too demanding and overactive, this is not because of woman's freedom. These things come, rather, from frustration and self-doubt. They are not to be cured by turning the clock back a hundred years, even if we could.

It ought not to be necessary to say that it is not unfeminine to be intelligent, to use one's head, to have deep interests. Leaving aside biological functions, real femininity does not consist any longer in what one does; it consists rather in the way one does things. It may be granted that our society, unlike others, France, for example, does not have any prominent image of a type of woman who is very, very feminine and very intelligent, highly educated and highly cultivated. But I see no reason why we cannot create one.

It is because of a lack of clarity about these matters that many of our most able young women waste their time, or use it inefficiently, at jobs far below the level of their abilities, while the need for trained people, particularly in the fields of health, education and welfare, grows every year more acute.

The problem is even more serious in the case of the girl who is sure that she wants to be a full-time homemaker. It is not only that she is taking on a job that requires more wisdom, more depth and breadth of understanding than most professional ones; the nation depends more and more heavily upon women of her type for maintaining a high level of culture and humanitarianism. Her education could not be neglected for long without a serious deterioration in our national fabric.

                    o   o   o

VIEWPOINT

The Concept of Success in Our Culture

BY SIMON S. OLSHANSKY

Clyde Kluckhohn states that a society is a structure of expectancies. And for most Americans success with the associated symbols of wealth and prestige is one of the expectancies, for in our society, as Kluckhohn points out, the worship of success has gone farther than in any known culture, save possibly pre-war Japan.

Briefly, what are the chance of success? Is success the result of ability, hard work, luck, or family connections?

Noland and Bakke in their field study report that ". . . the degree of equality of opportunity open to persons possessing identical qualifications contains a large element of luck at best. . . . If luck is a large ingredient of opportunity, the latter is certainly undependable and scarcely a condition upon which can be premised an assumption that the fittest survive and the best receive the highest rewards."

Reynolds and Shister conclude on the basis of another field study that "Most companies hope and believe that all new employees have a chance to advance, and that over the course of the years most of them will actually advance to higher positions. This hope is apparently fulfilled for only a minority of the work force. The remainder, whether because of lack of vacancies or personal inadequacies, remain at about the level at which they started." They further report that "A more disturbing prospect is that, even with ideal placement facilities, there will be a good deal of initiative and ambition which cannot be used in modern industry."

Tausing and Joslyn on the basis of a study of business leaders in 1932 wrote: "Here is definite evidence, then, that the present generation of American business leaders has been recruited in greater part from sons of business men, and only to a minor extent from the sons of farmers and manual laborers." And they pointed out that the trend in that direction was ever increasing.

And indeed their prediction was validated. In *Fortune* (November 1952) a study of 900 top executives reveals that "The typical big company top executive was born the son of a business man. . . ." Only 2.5 per cent of the 900 had fathers who were laborers. On the other hand 15 per cent of the group had fathers who were professional men and nearly 26 per cent had fathers who were

This article is reprinted with permission from the *Personnel and Guidance Journal,* XXXII (1954), 355-6.

founders or executives of companies. In short, it would appear that most of the executives are tending to come increasingly from the economically comfortable families.

° ° °

Striving for success, aside from other problems, produces an ethics not especially healthy from a personal or community point of view. Though Shepherd Mead[1] writes with tongue in cheek there is considerable truth underlying his Machiavellian (and humorous) suggestions for climbing the ladder of success.

" 'What's in it for me?' and 'What can I get out of it?' are guiding principles of too many people who educate themselves like a burglar preparing for a safe robbery by acquiring sharp and powerful tools to crack the bank of opportunity." And too often as a consequence integrity becomes subsidiary to what Erich Fromm aptly calls a marketable personality.

The final question and challenge: "If we demand that a man must succeed to be regarded as good, how difficult do we dare to make that success without running the risk of breaking the hearts and minds of many who fail?"

---

[1] Shepherd Mead, *How to Succeed in Business without Really Trying* (New York: Simon & Schuster, 1953).

CHAPTER 4

What are the Typical Problems of Freshmen?

COLLEGE PROBLEMS AND HIGH SCHOOL PROBLEMS

The college student, like the high school student, faces many difficult challenges. He too must try to find answers to his questions. He too must make his own choices.

The problems of college students are often strikingly similar to those of high school students. For example, many college students worry because they do things they later regret; so do high school students. College students often feel a lack of self-confidence. They find it difficult to concentrate. They may panic when taking tests. They are anxious to make friends and to be popular. They wonder what life is all about. And so do high school students.

Other problems of college students differ to some extent from those of high school students. The college student wants desperately to be independent. He refuses to be "treated like a child" any more. Yet he has actually gained some measure of the independence the high school student seeks, although he now finds his independence tempered by the responsibilities that go with it. The college student must make the decision as to the occupation he will pursue; the high school student was free to dream. The college student is often under severe pressure to do well in his studies. Pressures on high school students are considerably less, for the competition is not as intense and the consequences of failure not as serious. Under close analysis the difference between the problems of college and high school students turn out to be a matter of degree rather than kind.

Freshmen often come to college with an overly optimistic picture of what life will be like once they arrive. Some look forward to a glamorous social life at a kind of country club inhabited by beautiful girls and football heroes, strolling hand in hand without a care in the world. Other freshmen come with a grimly serious educational purpose. They ex-

> *Yet from the first crude days of settling time*
> *In this untried abode,*
> *I was disturbed at times by prudent thoughts,*
> *Wishing to hope without a hope, some fears*
> *About my future worldly maintenance,*
> *And, more than all, a strangeness in the mind,*
> *A feeling that I was not for that hour,*
> *Not for that place.*
>
> —William Wordsworth

pect to join a community composed only of dedicated scholars, with professors who can keep them perpetually enthralled and stimulated. Some freshmen are sure that they will spend the happiest years of their lives at dear old "Venusberg U."

All too often, the realities of college life do not match the image. College facilities, social life, and intellectual standards may not come up to the expectations of the freshman, and, instead of enjoying carefree times, he may sometimes find himself frustrated and unhappy. Nevertheless, nearly half of the freshmen questioned in one study agreed that their first year had been very satisfactory and they were enthusiastic about life in college (1). They had met new challenges and adjusted to new experiences. They enjoyed their new freedoms and responsibilities. They adapted to new and less personal methods of teaching, and they found out that their preparation for college was adequate, after all:

> College is great! My roommate is wonderful and it was easier to make friends than I thought. The other kids were just as anxious as I was to make friends, too.
>
> My high school teachers used to nag us to death. At first it seemed the instructors in college didn't care whether we did our work or not. It took me a while to learn that I had to do the work anyhow.
>
> It was wonderful to be on my own at last. I made plenty of mistakes but at least they were my own.
>
> I can honestly say that college taught me to think. I found out that other people had some of the same problems I have. I also found out that there is more to education than just preparing for a career.

Even though most college students are relatively happy, serious, and purposeful, they may complain about the increasing impersonality, the intense competition, and the stresses and pressures.

In contrast, some freshmen are very dissatisfied with many aspects of college. Some are unhappy because they feel that the college's standards are too low. Others complain that standards are too high. They may find themselves poorly prepared academically for the accelerated pace of college. Some students find their greatest difficulties in making emotional adjustments. Others are most concerned about their place in the social life of the campus:

> I never should have come to a technical school. For the life of me I can't figure out what I'm doing here. Maybe I would do better somewhere else.
>
> The courses here are a waste of time. Either I already know the stuff or else it's something I don't want to hear about.
>
> This college is a joke. The catalog said, "an intellectual atmosphere" but all I found was a bunch of ignorant phonies running around trying to impress each other.
>
> I don't think I'm fitted for college. I feel left out here. At home I used to be the center of attention. Now when I come home I'm a stranger there, too.
>
> They never give us enough time to do the reading to prepare these long reports. Every professor thinks his course is the only one I'm taking.
>
> The exams are horrible. They expect you to remember what they

talked about a month ago and then to build some fancy theory on it.

My high school counselor gave me the worst advice of all. He relied solely on my college examination scores.

I never imagined what a "rat-race" college would turn out to be.

Another personal problem of the college freshman relates to his new position in the campus hierarchy. He may have been the outstanding scholar in his own local high school but at college he finds that half of his class were valedictorians back home. He may have been a star athlete when he was in high school and yet be unable to place on the third string of the freshman squad. Only later does he come to realize that such drastic changes in status are inevitable as one progresses from one social level to another. The army top sergeant who becomes an officer quickly finds he has become only the lowliest among the second lieutenants.

One of the most desirable effects of college should be to give the student a realistic appraisal of himself, but many students complain that their advisers have no time to help them do so. The following comments of freshmen seem to show certain inadequacies of self-appraisal.

I think I would make a good teacher because I love children. I don't know why none of my instructors like me.

When I get to be a big success in business, I'll be able to hire other people to write letters for me.

I expect to be a doctor and naturally I have no interest in math or chemistry.

My adviser doesn't know me from Adam. How could he help me know my weaknesses?

Students who belong to the so-called minority groups sometimes face special personal problems in college. The chief peril is that of succumbing to the stereotyped viewpoint of the majority so that one comes to believe what "everyone else believes," even about his own group (6).

College students report that they face many specific problems during their first year (2). Some of these problems relate to their studies, some relate to their choice of a career, some to their social life, and some are personal. The important thing to keep in mind is that all students have problems. Indeed, everyone alive has problems. What counts is how effectively the person deals with them.

By seeing some examples of the worries and concerns of others, you may be helped to identify and come to terms with your own problems. It may also be reassuring to learn that you are not alone in your difficulties.

STUDENTS MEET ACADEMIC PROBLEMS

Many freshmen find that they are poorly prepared for college work. Not only have they learned too little in high school, but they also find that they lack the skills necessary for learning more in college. Academic difficulties such as these cause about one-third of all dropouts from college (3).

In order to survive, students must learn to listen to lectures and take intelligent and readable notes. They must learn to prepare assignments carefully and yet manage their time skillfully enough for other obligations. Students must learn to concentrate and to resist distractions. They must learn the skills of writing a term paper: choosing a topic, collecting and organizing data, and preparing an acceptable manuscript. Above all, they must learn to take different types of examinations covering long periods of study.

Students frequently encounter academic surprises in college. It is usually a more bookish world than many students expected. They are left on their own much more than they were in high school. Teachers may know little about their backgrounds and plans, and may not even know their names. Classes are often very large and there is much more lecturing than recitation. Since they were accustomed to more frequent progress reports, students are sometimes disturbed because they do not know where they stand.

I was able to breeze through high school just by using common sense. I don't do that in this place.

Students frequently blame the college, their teachers, their high school, or themselves for their difficulties.

Why don't the colleges and the high schools ever get together and straighten out the overlapping and the gaps between the curriculums?

College is just a glorified high school. I'm still taking a bunch of courses I don't want and I don't need.

Many students starting college, especially those who are vocationally oriented, expect to plunge immediately into the heart of their pet subjects. They are disappointed and discouraged by the mass of requirements and by what seem to be unrelated subjects they must take before they get into their major field of interest. Thus, many students believe that their main academic problem results from being forced to take courses without understanding why. They see little relevance between their goals and the freshman courses they are required to take. Moreover, they cannot find any interrelationships among the various courses. Some freshmen resent having to take any required courses. They feel they are old enough and experienced enough to select their academic program.

I always thought that I would be able to choose my own courses once I got to college. Now I find that I get three hours of electives and the rest of my time is spent in dreary required subjects. I just can't see any connections.

Many students are dissatisfied with the increasing compartmentalization and fragmentation of knowledge.

Things are changing so fast that I expect everything I learn will be out of date before I'm finished.

Most important of all the academic problems is the intense pressure for high grades at most colleges. Students find themselves in fierce competition with other students and even worse, in competition with the instructor by trying to outwit him instead of learning from him. Emphasis turns to getting the grades at any cost: intensive cramming, searching for minimum test responses that will be marked correct, all accompanied by a great deal of tension and frantic activity.

At this college, students keep books out of the library just so other students can't get them ...
I studied just what I thought he'd ask but he crossed us up.
I hate this business of grade-grabbing but how else can you get anywhere?
Efficiency is much more important than excellence. This place is run like a factory.

In a desperate effort to improve their grades, some students resort to various forms of dishonesty ranging from stealing footnotes on term papers to falsifying sources and cheating on examinations. This leads to severe struggles of conscience for some. Others rationalize.

Everybody cheats on exams. If I didn't, I would come out second-best ...
I wish someone would stop these cheaters but I'm not the one to do it.

Another effect of the pressure for high grades is serious overwork for some students. Even the better students sometimes drive themselves too hard. Fatigue accumulates, efficiency drops, and the student finds himself at the point of physical exhaustion. In later chapters of this book, attention will be given to the practical improvement of academic performance through more efficient use of study skills.

Many college freshmen have academic problems in college because they lacked serious intentions or realistic goals while they were in high school. These students may be classified as follows:

"New-leafers"

believed that everything in college would be entirely different from high school. They thought they would suddenly change from indifferent high school students to brilliant college scholars. They would get a completely fresh start and not be expected to remember anything dreary from the past. But they are dismayed to find that college is, to some extent, a continuation of high school, and much of the subject matter is quite similar. To their sorrow, they often find that slovenly study habits are difficult to break, and they cannot really turn over the new leaf and start afresh.

"Stepping-stoners"

look upon college as merely a means to a specific goal. For example, some girls go to college only to find a husband. Some boys go to college until they are old enough to enter a family business. Some may wish to play professional football and hope to catch the eye of a scout. Such students rarely prepare themselves seriously while in high school because they do not expect to take college seriously. They find that college stubbornly resists being used as just a stepping-stone.

"Drifters"

pass through high school without getting seriously involved and come to college because they cannot think of any other place to go. Sometimes, fortunately, these students find a worthy purpose for themselves in college; but they are nevertheless handicapped by their wasted opportunities while in high school.

"Last-minutemen"

had no expectation of going to college. They are anxious to leave school, to gain economic independence, and to free themselves from restrictions. For them, high school may have been associated with childish routines.

When they begin looking for their place in the world, they find the labor market glutted with other hopeful but unprepared workers like themselves. Some then turn to college but must reorient themselves to an environment they intended to escape.

VOCATIONAL CHOICES CREATE PROBLEMS

"What are you going to be when you grow up?"

This question has been with the student ever since childhood when he first began to dream of a glamorous position in life. Over the years he has probably changed his vocational goals many times without much consequence, but now it seems that a permanent decision must be reached all at once. Pressures to make a choice come from various directions—from the student's parents, from the college, and from the student himself. The student is eager to identify with a field which will gain him respect and security. His parents want him to "be somebody" and usually feel that this is the main reason they are sending their child to college. The college often begins by asking the student to choose his "major," a choice which is related to an ultimate occupational goal.

In response to these pressures, a student may reach a hasty and unwise vocational decision which is not in keeping with his own achievements, abilities, interests, or aptitudes. Once a decision is reached, changing to another vocational choice then becomes progressively more difficult, time-consuming, and expensive. Proper vocational guidance in advance can help reduce the danger of making an unsuitable decision.

SOCIAL LIFE MAY RESULT IN DILEMMAS

Everything seems to happen at once to the college freshman. He may face social situations which are unlike anything in his past experience. For example, the varying cultural backgrounds of other students and their wide range of values and attitudes may be a surprise to him. Even such relatively minor matters as differences in dress, manners, and speech may be disturbing to some freshmen. Most students, however, take these new experiences in stride; they may even enjoy them. Others are more rigid and are upset when they find social realities quite different from their expectations.

Even though students are friendly to each other, college can still be a cold, hard place. There seems to be something missing which is hard to explain.

I have yet to find *anywhere* or *anyplace* or *anytime* in which you can be alone. For instance, you're in your room, and you put out a "DO NOT DISTURB" sign, and people come in to find out why you don't want to be disturbed.

Freshmen report, for example, that they have difficulty in meeting so many new people, making new friends, finding and identifying with social groups, choosing sororities and fraternities, dating, and getting along with roommates. They are concerned with morals and values, and the responsibility of making their own decisions. Finding a congenial group is difficult for some entering freshmen, while others are dissatisfied with the friends they have made:

I don't seem to fit in anywhere. I always looked forward to the social life at college and I never thought I would have trouble making friends. I thought by going to a large school I'd meet and know more people. I don't even know the students in my own dorm.

Some students place a great value upon acceptance by a particular *sorority or fraternity*. To be left out is a great blow and often one they cannot face:

The Greeks run the show here and if you're not one of them you might as well hang up. I'm not one of them.

On the other hand, students who do join sororities and fraternities generally like the security and identity of belonging but sometimes complain about excessive demands upon their time, the superficial value system, and the pointlessness of many of their activities (4).

Dating presents many problems to college students and is a very common source of their anxieties. There are constant pressures to date and to be considered popular. The date itself is often a kind of contest, with both participants afraid of giving too much or receiving too little. The whole intricate process is then analyzed and discussed by the friends of the contestants.

For many students, the problem of moral standards is closely tied to the problem of dating. Some are reluctant to make their own decisions and bear their own responsibilities, not only in the area of dating but in other areas of daily life as well. Many students are confused by the norms of behavior. They find themselves making shaky compromises which frequently are in conflict with the teachings of their church, their home, and their own deeper beliefs.

I really don't care for all this making out, but if you don't, a boy won't ask you again . . .

I decided that I would have to live with myself long after I left my

college friends. Sometimes it's hard to stick to my standards, but I'm trying . . .

This place is so full of different kinds of heads that when I smile they all want to know what I'm on.

Students learn a great deal from each other. Some even say they can learn more outside the classroom than in it. Orientation to fellow students is definitely part of the educational experience. Much of what you learn in college—for better or worse—comes from other students.

On many campuses there is much pressure on the individual student to conform to one of the campus models of behavior. Some students have a great need for "belonging" and get their feelings of security from their group identification, while some students want independence at all costs. Both kinds of students are found at most campuses. Although a certain amount of adjustment to local college mores may be necessary, each student must decide for himself how much of campus life he can accept and how much he must reject. Adjustment to the wrong prevailing values is the beginning of the end.

True independence of thought is, of course, not easy to maintain in the face of pressures to conform. Even "non-conformists" often fall into their own group social patterns and these may become as rigid as the conventional ones. A group of male students dressed identically, even to the same hair style, was once heard to agree that they could not stand wearing a uniform. A comedian summed up this pattern of behavior: "I want to be different—just like everyone else."

Keep in mind that a college student is a person in the process of change, for to be educated is to be changed. The college experience becomes more meaningful for the student if he is conscious of the changes and is prepared for them. Even the frustrations and disappointments of college life are a part of the educational process, and some educators are convinced that it is only by overcoming frustration that we can make any experience truly our own.

MANY PROBLEMS ARE PERSONAL

One of the most important problems freshmen face is the necessity of getting to know themselves realistically. Students who are poorly adjusted to college may grossly overestimate or underestimate their own abilities and aptitudes. Many freshmen who withdraw or who are asked to leave college go through the entire year believing somehow that their work is satisfactory. On the other hand, some excellent students worry needlessly throughout their college years.

College students want to become independent adults, to throw off the shackles of childhood and adolescence, but they are only partially prepared to take this giant step. They may find the responsibilities of life on their own to be a constant source of tension. They just cannot handle all of their new obligations such as writing home, keeping appointments, and taking care of themselves and their possessions.

Most college students undergo changes in their relationship to their families. Sometimes these changes are very drastic and disturbing to everyone concerned. But usually students are able to assume independence gradually and parents are able to accept the fact. Some students who are unable to adjust to their new responsibilities persist in calling upon their parents to make the decisions. Others seek and find substitute parents on campus to do this.

Homesickness is a frequent problem among students who are away from home for the first time. Often, however, this may be only the outward symptom of some underlying problem (5). Such personal emotional problems are a common cause of dropouts from college.

A student may return from college and find that, in effect, he has become a stranger to his own father and mother. American novels and biographies contain many examples of this sort of experience. On the other hand, students may return to gain a new appreciation of their parents as human beings. Mark Twain once remarked that when he was fourteen he thought his father was pretty ignorant but that when he was twenty-one he was surprised at how much the old man had learned in the past seven years!

Many students finally gain a measure of independence from parental authority only to substitute the more arbitrary authority of their own group. They talk independence but practice conformity. Above all, they fear loneliness and isolation, and to protect themselves they imitate the accepted manners, morals, speech, and thought of the campus leaders (6). More often than not, such leaders are themselves models of conformity to the crowd. One is reminded of the story of a mob marching down the streets of Paris during the Revolution. Following the crowd is one man. When asked why he is marching, he replies, "I have to follow them. I am their leader."

THE PROBLEM OF CONTINUING IN COLLEGE

It is not uncommon for students to question whether they are in the right college or whether they belong in college at all. Some decide to leave because of their initial disappointments and frustrations.

One reason for leaving school is that the student may be attending a college which is truly wrong for him. His parents may have chosen his college unrealistically: because it was private, or because it was small, distant, or expensive. Some parents insist upon a "prestige college" at all costs. Some insist that their child attend a college under denominational control despite the wishes and interests of the student himself. Most students do best when they attend a college which they have helped to choose. Even acceptance at a college or university does not mean that the college is *right* for the individual student. Colleges vary in their academic and social climates, in their strengths and limitations. A student may perform poorly in one setting yet succeed in another.

This place is not for me. I was taken in by the catalogue descriptions.

I was told that one place is as good as another, that it was all up to me. I know differently now.

Around here I'm running on four cylinders in an eight cylinder society. I am trying to find the courage to transfer to an easier school.

At best, there is no perfect choice of a college, for the colleges themselves are everchanging institutions. Unfortunately, chances for failure are increased by the frequently haphazard manner in which the original selection was made.

PROBLEMS CAN BE SOLVED

Ultimately each person must solve his own problems. He can choose to ignore them for a while, to run away from them, or to face up to them and to make the necessary changes. He can also learn to put up with circumstances that cannot be changed. If he chooses, he can seek help from his friends, his parents, or his counselors.

Many students drift along and do not bother to face the responsibilities of going to college. Some merely enjoy the nonacademic pleasures of the campus until suddenly it is too late to prepare for examinations. Behind the majority of such college failures are undefined emotional problems and a failure to seek help in sufficient time. Yet ignoring problems sometimes works. One may become accustomed in time to the most unpleasant situation, or, if one waits, other people may make the decisions. A man who cannot decide whether to stay in college or join the army may find that a board composed of his friends and neighbors has made the decision for him.

Running away from problems may take many forms: overactivity, drinking, sexual promiscuity, psychosomatic illness, or even complete withdrawal. Another form of running away is simply to leave college altogether, without any realistic thought or planning.

The college student who is emotionally mature can appraise his own situation realistically, weighing both the positive and negative factors. He can evaluate his own strengths and weaknesses and he deliberately tries to increase his skills for learning. In the process of learning how to adjust himself to the situation, he makes use of whatever help is available. He realizes that as Robert Frost pointed out, "a college education consists of hanging around until you've caught on (7)."

Most colleges today offer counseling services to help students solve their problems. But many students fail to make use of these services because they misunderstand the function of the counselor. The duty of the counselor is to help the student arrive at his own decisions, not to make the decisions for him; to help the student solve his own problems, not to solve the problems for him; to help the student explore possible goals and possible courses of action, not to plan the student's life for him.

College counselors normally have a large amount of information about a student. They have his past academic records and data on the entrance or guidance tests he may have taken. In addition, they have contact with all of his teachers. Most important, they have the training and experience to help him to clarify and evaluate all of this diverse information.

One point of attack on a common problem of the student is an effort to improve his study habits directly. Some suggestions for accomplishing this are given in the next part of this book.

NOTES TO CHAPTER 4

(1) Agatha Townsend, *College Freshmen Speak Out* (New York: Harper & Row, 1956), pp. 112f.

(2) Many students who have failed in one college seek a second chance in the junior college. Such students are required to file a petition showing causes for their previous poor performance in college. From a random sample of student petitions for admission to the Fall Term, 1962, at Wright College in Chicago, have emerged five broad categories of reasons given by the students for failure in college work.

   A. *Improper adjustment to college* includes the problems arising from the student's first experiences in living away from home, meeting the demands of preparation for college classes and trying to cope with the large scale operations of college. Female students eighteen to nineteen years old and students of both sexes who were in the upper one-fourth of their high school classes were prominent among those who said they failed because of this problem.

   B. *Personal problems* include the student's illness, hostility of parents, financial difficulties necessitating employment, and emotional upsets. Such problems were cited as reasons for failure by all groups of students in the sample.

C. *Immaturity and poor attitude toward the importance of college education* are more often given by the men students than by the women as sources of difficulty.

D. *Lack of motivation and interest* is revealed by certain frank statements from the students that they had no real interest in college work or that they were uncertain of goals and found themselves following the wrong curriculum. The male students are predominant in attributing their failure to this cause, especially those eighteen and nineteen years old. This problem, however, was common to both sexes ranked in the lower one-fourth of their high school classes.

E. *Poor study habits and poor study environment* reflect both the student's admission of lack of application and his complaints concerning crowded dormitory and library conditions. These causes of failure were common to all students.

     The sample produced other evidence concerning the students who are seeking readmission to college after initial failure:

A. The largest group of women who petitioned for admission were eighteen to nineteen years old, indicating that the first year of college is the greatest test for them. This conclusion is supported by the fact that these women indicated improper college adjustment as their greatest source of difficulty.

B. The fact that the number of men petitioning for admission in the eighteen-to-nineteen-year group was approximately equal to the number in the group twenty and above suggests that the test of college ability and performance for men continues for a longer period than it does for women. The poor study habits, poor preparation, and interference from employment which are most frequently mentioned by the men may even increase in their detrimental effects upon college performance as men reach the second or third year.

    From William C. Resnick and William D. Jordan, "A Second Chance: A Review of Petitions for Admission," Unpublished research study (Chicago: Wright Junior College, 1962).

(3) Nevitt Sanford, *The American College*, pp. 631f.

(4) Annelies A. Rose, "A Study of College Freshmen," *Journal of Social Psychology*, XXVI (1947), 195ff.

    Many personality factors were found to be related to homesickness at Smith College. Those most homesick were often poorly adjusted, showed greater anxiety, and were more socially inept. They also tended to come from homes where they were more dominated by their parents.

(5) David Riesman, *Individualism Reconsidered* (Glencoe, Illinois: The Free Press, 1954).

(6) See, for example: Kurt Lewin, *Resolving Social Conflicts* (New York: Harper and Row, 1948), chap. 12.

(7) *Philadelphia Inquirer* (January 30, 1963) as cited in Martha Wright, "Ad Eundem Gradum" *AAUP Bulletin*. LII, 4 (December, 1966), p. 433.

SUGGESTIONS FOR FURTHER READING

Bell, Norman T., Robert W. Burkhardt, and Victor B. Lawhead, *Introduction to College Life* (2nd ed.). Boston: Houghton Mifflin Co., 1966.

Blaine, Graham B. and Charles C. McArthur, *Emotional Problems of College Students.* New York: Appleton-Century-Crofts, 1961.

Cook, F. J., *Youth in Danger,* New York: Harcourt, Brace & World, Inc., 1956.

Crowne, Leslie Joan, *Adjustment Problems of College Freshmen,* New York: Teachers College, Columbia University, 1955.

Goldsen, Rose K., Morris Rosenberg, Robin M. Williams, Jr., and Edward A. Suchman, *What College Students Think.* Princeton, New Jersey: D. Van Nostrand Co., Inc., 1960.

Havemann, Ernest and Patricia Salter West, *They Went to College.* New York: Harcourt, Brace & World, Inc., 1952.

Hutchins, Robert M., *Education for Freedom.* Baton Rouge, La.: Louisiana University Press, 1943.

Jacob, Phillip, *Changing Values in College.* New York: Harper & Row, 1958.

Landes, Paul H., *So This Is College.* New York: McGraw-Hill Book Company, 1954.

Lee, A. M., *Fraternities Without Brotherhood, A Study of Prejudice.* Boston: Beacon Press, 1955.

Lindner, R., *Must You Conform?* New York: Holt, Rinehart and Winston, Inc., 1962.

Riesman, David, *Selected Essays from Individualism Reconsidered.* Garden City, New York: Doubleday Anchor Books (A58), 1955.

————————— with Nathan Glazer and Reuel Denney, *The Lonely Crowd.* Garden City, New York: Doubleday Anchor Books (A16), 1953.

Rivlin, Harry N., and others, *First Years in College.* Boston: Houghton Mifflin Co., 1965.

SOME FICTIONAL WORKS PORTRAYING
PROBLEMS OF YOUNG PEOPLE

Baldwin, James, *Go Tell It On the Mountain.* New York: Alfred A. Knopf, Inc., 1953, pp. 46-50. (Some good and bad ways of adjusting, showing how one displaces his anger on to other people.)

Bunin, Ivan, *The Well of Days.* New York: Alfred A. Knopf, Inc., 1934, pp. 227-231.

Canfield, Dorothy, *The Bent Twig.* New York: Henry Holt and Co., Inc., 1943, pp. 145-152. (Vivid portrayal of the impact of being rejected from joining a sorority.)

Dell, Floyd, *Moon-Calf.* New York: Doubleday and Co., Inc., 1920, pp. 181-183. (Portrays the feelings and difficulties when one feels out of place because of his background.

Eustis, Helen, *The Fool Killer.* New York: Doubleday and Co., Inc., 1954, pp. 169-179.

Frankau, Pamela, *A Wreath for the Enemy*. New York: Harper and Row, 1952, pp. 76-79 (Shows rebelliousness against one's family and feelings accompanying this action.)

Gide, Andre, *The Counterfeiters*. New York: Alfred A. Knopf, Inc. 1952, pp. 56-58. (Shows behavior towards others in an effort to prevent being hurt by them.)

Jackson, Shirley, *Hangsaman*. New York: Farrar, Straus and Cudahy, Inc., 1951, pp. 84-91. (Excellent example of the use of rationalization as a defense mechanism.)

Joyce, James, *A Portrait of the Artist as a Young Man*. New York: The Viking Press, 1944, pp. 236-240. (Interesting discussion of college problems and those who students feel are responsible for creating these problems.)

Marquand, John P., *So Little Time*. Boston: Little, Brown and Co., 1943, pp. 175-189. (Some of the difficulties involved in social adjustments.)

Maugham, W. Somerset, *Of Human Bondage*. New York: Doubleday and Co., Inc., 1936. (Excellent portrayal of the personal feelings involved in knowing that one is physically handicapped.)

Maxwell, William, *The Folded Leaf*. New York: Harper and Brothers, 1945. (Some problems inherent in growing up.)

Morton, Frederick, *Asphalt and Desire*. New York: Harcourt, Brace and World, Inc., 1952, pp. 68-72. (The problem of communication and understanding between the young person and his family.)

Rolland, Romain, *Jean Christophe*. New York: Henry Holt and Co., Inc., 1913. (Examples of the problems in self-understanding.)

Wells, H. G., *The Bulpington of Blup*. New York: The Macmillan Co., 1933, p. 334. (Examples of defensive mechanisms to satisfy needs and wants.)

Wolfe, Thomas, *Look Homeward, Angel*. New York: Charles Scribners' Sons, 1929, p. 596. (The need for identification and the search for it.)

VIEWPOINT

Students Look at College Education

BY ROSE K. GOLDSEN, MORRIS ROSENBERG,
ROBIN M. WILLIAMS, JR., AND EDWARD A. SUCHMAN

> *Do students generally believe their colleges are doing a
> good job?*
> *Do they see the college as an impersonal institution?*
> *What are the major criticisms students make about their
> college experiences?*
> *According to the students, what should be the goals of the
> college?*
> *Do the opinions of these students agree with your
> own opinions today? Explain.*

Today as never before students are flocking to the college campuses. Class-rooms are bulging, living facilities are severely taxed, qualified teaching person-nel are in short supply, and the competition for college space is the keenest in history. A college degree is no longer the privilege of a limited elite; in the United States higher education is rapidly becoming mass education.

The widening base of who is being educated raises important questions about assumptions that underlie fundamental policies of higher education. We wish to examine some of these assumptions among the student population. What do college students, themselves, feel and think about the kind of educational fare they are entitled to? How do they react to what they are getting? The students, after all, are the material the colleges have to work with. How, then, do the students approach the college experience? What does it mean to them?

"The Colleges are Doing a Good Job"

For context we begin with something as general as the students' frame of mind. It is decidedly approving. College students feel that college education is important, useful, and of good calibre. Their morale is high. They *like* going to college. They say their colleges and universities are doing a good job. They say that what they, themselves, are doing on the campuses is worthwhile and im-portant. In fact, we found only three topics in our entire study on which stu-dents showed such close agreement: that love is important in marriage; that religious freedom is essential in a democracy; and that the opportunity to go to college is important and meaningful.

Almost every student in our samples said "having the opportunity to go to college is very important to me." The vast majority say that "the colleges are doing a good job"; that "most of what I am learning in college is very worthwhile." Most students say that their own university is adequately meeting their educational standards. They feel that college education equips them for life outside the campus. They deny that their colleges are behind the times. Indeed, as many as 37 per cent have no misgivings about agreeing to the extreme view that "America has the best system of college education in the world."

When we asked the students to evaluate the university's role in educating for values, quite apart from the communication of subject matter, again their reactions showed high approval. The vast majority deny that they have found college to be in any way a disillusioning experience; only a handful say they have lost respect for college education. Nor does any substantial percentage agree with the kinds of criticisms sometimes voiced—that American colleges and college teachers place insufficient emphasis on teaching religious values or American ideals and values.

It is not solely that the students approve of their college education in general; they express feelings of loyalty to their own campuses and many even tend to personify their schools. They do not see an impersonal institution with a strictly educational function. They see a group that has "its own personality, something over and above the individual members in it." Indeed, when we asked these students to check any of eight different groups which they felt had this quality, "your college" led the list. More than family, more than church or religion, more than nation, the students feel that their college possesses this special quality of *personality* rather than *impersonality*.

Yet their overwhelming approval and strong identification by no means precludes certain serious criticisms of specific aspects of university life. The most widespread criticisms, however, are directed not toward the nature of the educational experience itself, but rather toward certain administrative policies which suggest tendencies toward an impersonal mass approach to education. Many of the students we polled said they felt that charges of "production-line teaching methods" are justified; that teachers are underpaid; that few or none of the professors take a personal interest in their students; that the colleges overemphasize athletics perhaps at the expense of academic interests.

The liberal or conservative atmosphere of the university is somewhat less likely to be a target for criticism. Yet it would distort the picture to gloss over the subgroups who criticize the colleges for racial or religious discrimination in admissions policy; who say that there is a suppression of academic freedom, and that college teachers "are afraid to say what they really believe these days." (. . . Ivy League colleges and the Northeastern men's colleges are least critical; the large Southern universities and Fisk seem to be more issue-conscious. But over-all approval, campus to campus, is marked.)

The students' overwhelming approval of many aspects of college education, then, does not indicate an unquestioning acceptance of anything and everything about college or university life. Their enthusiastic general evaluation does not prevent many of them from being critical of certain characteristics and practices that they say diminish the value of the educational experience and make the colleges fall short in certain important respects. Nor does it mean that their opinions can be viewed as competent evaluation of the sort of educational experience they are having. The point is that their morale is high, their spirit is good, their frame of mind is receptive. This is what is significant in the general agreement that "the colleges are doing a good job."

The goals of college education. "Doing a good job"—about what? What precisely are the tasks the university is expected to perform?

Most students feel that the university has not one job to do, but many, diverging principally in the relative emphasis they declare that each of these jobs deserves:

> Well, first and foremost, you have to prepare yourself for your career, your specialty. You can't have a real career without college, that's the first thing they ask you. But you should learn more than just your own field. Education in general, culture. You have to learn about ideas. You have to think critically. Not to accept things blindly. Another thing, when you come to college you meet many different kinds of people. One of the most important things is to learn how to get along with them. . . .

> I think it's important to broaden yourself culturally, to learn how to think. Of course it's important to prepare yourself for a job. But even an engineer has to write reports. And he should also know about citizenship and world problems. That's just as important as knowing how to build a bridge. . . .

> For me the most important thing about college is that I hope to prepare myself for marriage. I plan to marry as soon as I graduate. But I'll want to work after the children are old enough, so I definitely want to finish and get my degree. It will help me get a job, yes. But I think the things I learn here —not only in classes but also in hash sessions—will help me to do my main job which is to be a wife and mother. . . .

> Too many people seem to forget that in college you should be learning not only knowledge, but also how to live a full and meaningful life. There's more to life than your career. In college you should have an opportunity to clarify your ideas about morals and ethics, what you think is right and wrong. Important and unimportant in the "big" sense of the word.

Most of the students we talked to showed this tendency to list not one value of the college experience, but several, and to arrange them in a hierarchic order of importance.

o o o

The most generally accepted opinion is that college ought to provide "a basic general education and appreciation of ideas." Since this approach to college education is intrinsic in academic educational tradition, we shall, for the sake of brevity, refer to this alternative as an indicator of an academic set of educational values. This approach is emphasized by a substantial majority of the students: 74 per cent rated it highly important.

The view that college ought to "develop your ability to get along with all kinds of people" focuses upon the importance of social and interpersonal skills. For this reason we refer to this alternative as an indicator of "interpersonal" educational values. The interpersonal emphasis in higher education appears to be about as widespread as the academic: 72 per cent said they considered it highly important.

The opinion that college ought to provide "vocational training, . . . skills and techniques directly applicable to your career," stresses the value of college as a means to a given end. Again, for the sake of brevity, we refer to this alternative as an indicator of instrumental educational values, an approach which is considered highly important by 60 per cent of the students.

Student opinion seems to focus mainly on these three approaches to higher education. It is equally important, however, to observe that large proportions say that the other goals of college education are also weighty. Fifty per cent stress the university's role in training for citizenship; 45 per cent rate the moral functions of university training as highly important. These are the less popular goals of education, but they are still emphasized by many of the students. Only the family-training role of the university is likely to be rejected by considerable numbers.

The climate of opinion varies in certain characteristic ways, campus to campus. For example, students at the Eastern men's colleges with a relatively long tradition behind them (Harvard, Yale, Wesleyan, Dartmouth) are least likely to stress vocational education and most likely to emphasize "basic general education and appreciation of ideas." At Wesleyan—a denominational campus—they are more likely to stress "moral capacities, ethical standards and values." There seems to be a certain tendency for opinions to be "tailored," as it were, to the distinctive environment of each individual campus. . . .

But the students evaluate an "ideal" college education by applying several sets of standards simultaneously. All these standards may genuinely be considered "highly" important. What do they say they feel deserves higher education's principal emphasis?

We can approximate an answer to this question by looking at the . . . educational goals which were ranked as *the* single most important aim of an ideal university. The majority of students stress either a "basic general education and appreciation of ideas," or "vocational skills and techniques directly applicable to your career." Thirty-five per cent and 36 per cent, respectively, select these as "the single most important" aim of an ideal university. Still the proportion who place primary emphasis on the interpersonal approach to higher education is substantial enough (17 per cent) to preclude the possibility of misunderstanding, or the whimsical entry of a check mark. The other aims of education we have been discussing turn out to be clearly secondary. But "getting along with people"—as many observers of American culture have remarked and deplored—is certainly considered a legitimate purpose of higher education by a discernible sub-group of the students.

But this generalization turns out to be an accurate description principally of the beginning students. Academic educational values, more than any of the others we are discussing, are the ones whose claim to legitimacy seems to become reinforced on the campuses we studied, as the students mature.

As the students pass through their colleges, certain of the educational values they profess shift position in the hierarchy of all educational values considered important. Thus, just as the climate of opinion on the most desirable educational goals varies from campus to campus, it varies as well from college class to college class. Upper classmen, for example, almost unanimously place primary emphasis on academic or vocational education: the interpersonal approach drops to a position of secondary importance. Seniors may still view the opportunity to develop skills in interpersonal relations as perhaps a fortunate by-product of the college years, but the proportion who consider this approach important enough to deserve principal attention declines in the final year of college. It is mainly in the earlier years that such an approach has primary value for any significant proportion of the college students.

The changing climate of opinion year by year is apparent in another important sense. In the freshmen and sophomore classes, the opinion that vocational education should be the most important aim of college education takes precedence over all others. Among juniors, emphasis on vocational education or general education as principal aims of education is about equally balanced. But in the senior year, the point of view that college ought to provide chiefly a "basic education and appreciation of ideas" is far more prevalent than any other.

o   o   o

VIEWPOINT

How to Stay in College
BY ROBERT U. JAMESON

*What is the major problem of freshmen, according to all
college deans who were interviewed?*
*What is the major difference between high school and
college?*
*What should a freshman do if he gets into academic dif-
ficulty?*
What is the most important cause for freshman failure?
What are other common problems of freshmen?

. . . Although they may state it differently, all college deans from coast to
coast agree on one point: The major problem of the college freshmen is that of
adjusting to a new kind of life, in which he is expected to behave like an adult.
. . . In one way or another, what happens in the first year or two of college depends largely upon this one thing: Is the college student ready to grow up, to
understand what college is?

What is college? By the end of this article, I believe that the question will be
answered fairly. To begin with, here are some general statements about what
college is. Robert B. Cox, Dean of Men at Duke University, says that his fer-
vent wish is to be able some day to prove to an entering class that the freshman year is not Grade 13 in high school. Father Edward Dwyer, of Villanova
College, says this: "I wish that it were possible for us to demonstrate that college is a place for adults, not an advanced school for children." And a young
man who has just finished his first year at Princeton says this: "The most
important problems facing a freshman are those of adjustment to a unique
society, one totally different from high school."

Can college be defined?

In the first place, college is a place in which a person can learn how to learn.
In school, boys and girls are taught something about how to pass courses in
order to get a school diploma. Often enough they get the diploma at a certain
age even with a record of failure. In college, on the other hand, these boys
and girls are asked to learn to think, to meet complex intellectual problems
and to handle these problems on their own. Intellectual independence, the first
requisite of college, is often a distinct shock to a freshman.

An example of one college's method will perhaps make the point clearer.
At the Carnegie Institute of Technology, English composition courses are quite
unlike highschool courses. Students may be given several opposing points of

---

Mr. Jameson has served with the College Entrance Examination Board. This article is
reprinted from *The Saturday Evening Post*, October 2, 1954, by permission of the author.

view about a single topic and told to reach a logical, unbiased conclusion in a composition about this topic. The unwary freshman is thus faced with the necessity of using logic, of discarding personal prejudices and of writing carefully in order to prove to his instructor that he is capable of thinking through a problem. This "case-study" method is used in more than one freshman course in college.

o   o   o

How do freshmen react to situations like these? Unfortunately, many will react badly because the spoon feeding of the high school, the parents eager to help with homework, the teacher who leads classes by the nose are all missing. Now the human brain, perhaps the least-used muscle in the human body, has to start working on its own.

o   o   o

When the 1,000,000 new freshmen arrive for Freshman Week at any of the nearly 2,000 colleges in the land, they are put through a complicated and sometimes bewildering mill. They meet their roommates. They meet their advisers. They take placement tests and aptitude tests and reading tests and physical examinations. They meet the president. They are invited to buy the school paper, pennants, beer mugs, rugs, laundry service and everything else under the sun. They attend a football rally and chapel and a dance or two and a picnic and a number of meetings for indoctrination in the methods of study.

They are breezed through a very pleasant week—dizzying, perhaps, but new and different. They don't even have time to get homesick. That comes about two weeks later. Now, during this week, deans and advisers say many things which freshmen may, to their sorrow, ignore:

Start studying at once.

Get to know the library immediately.

Set up a schedule for yourself—revise it later, if necessary—to include both social and academic activities.

Join one or two extracurricular activities, but not every one in sight.

Get enough sleep.

Don't forget chapel.

Don't cut classes.

You're on your own; make the most of your independence.

But if you get into trouble, see your adviser right away.

Then classes begin, and the realities of college are suddenly all too evident. The first theme is written; the first history test is taken; the first physics experiment is done. And the first blast comes from a teacher, who, unlike lovable old Mr. Chips at home in the high school, is apparently half devil and half dragon.

o   o   o

A freshman's reaction to failure is a clear indication of whether he is a child or an adult. The adult simply works harder. The child may get surly. He may blame the instructor, not realizing that it is he, not the instructor, who has failed. He may look for excuses to explain his failure—headaches, a loud-mouthed roommate, the radio across the hall.

Because the college is concerned about the student who is in trouble and wants to save him, elaborate counseling programs have been set up in every college. The counselors, or advisers, try first to find out why students fail and then try to correct the trouble.

Among the causes for freshman failure, certainly the most important is lack of adequate training in secondary school. Overworked and underpaid teachers are simply not finding it possible to condition many of their students for the rigors of college work, particularly in the one most important subject of all: English.

According to almost every administrative officer in the colleges, the average freshman is deficient in the basic skills of reading and composition. Poor reading is usually caused by lack of practice. The average student today simply does not read many books; consequently, when he has to face long and complicated reading assignments in college, he may find that he has to study forty or fifty hours a week to keep his head above water. Or he may throw up his hands, say the assignments are impossible and go on to the movies. In the latter case he will probably be on probation before long.

                              o   o   o

The student who ... [has] trouble ... [with reading] should ... at least go over the problem with his adviser, who will be able to give sound advice about the art of studying.

A large number of young college men and women say that one of their most serious freshman-year mistakes was not seeing their advisers often enough.

If reading by freshmen is poor, composition is generally even worse. "Remedial English" and its counterparts in hundreds of colleges waste time doing highschool work while advanced work has to wait. But college students must be able to communicate an idea, whether in literature or physics. College advisers wish that all schools could somehow graduate all students with at least a rudimentary idea of what a good sentence is.

This description of poor preparation in English, which is commented on again and again in the colleges—a Harvard faculty report in 1898 made the complaint—is not intended to condemn the high school English teachers of America. Nor is it to be understood that every freshman is poorly prepared. The majority of freshmen have been in classes so large that no teacher can be expected to assign a weekly theme, much less correct the theme and confer with every student about the paper. Thus the freshman is too often in trouble because of shortcomings which have nothing to do with his ability. ...

The next academic problem of the freshman year—and this applies to all students, whether or not they have specific subject-matter difficulty—is that of how to study and how much to study.

                              o   o   o

... A hundred freshmen, at the end of the year, say the same thing: start to study at once. Don't get behind. "Boy, if I dropped a pencil in the lecture room, I missed a semester's work," said a Penn State Marine Corps veteran.

This "busting out," or flunking, by well-prepared, intelligent students is what the Dean of Freshmen at Duke calls the "G-Factor." G stands for

Goof, in the . . . slang use of the word. The bright boy who goofs is a very big headache to his college and a terrible waste of money, brains, effort and teaching. Obviously a number of these G-boys find themselves. What is tragic is that failure is the only way to show such a bright boy or girl that the college means business.

The jolt of failure sometimes produces results other than recovery. One common reaction is to blame the instructor. But no college adviser has much time for such an attitude. "I always tell characters like that," says a dean of a Southern college, "that I don't care what he thinks of the teacher. I tell him the library is right across the street. He can learn a lot there."

                                        o   o   o

But academic failure is by no means the only cause of trouble in college. Since college life is a complete and complicated existence, failure often comes to the student who cannot preserve the important balance between his academic and his social life. Overemphasis on extra-curricular activities, too much drinking, too much dating, too much fraternity activity—all of these will lead to trouble.

College, like life, is far too full of temptations. "My hardest job," says a bright young man, "was to take over where my parents left off—to learn to face facts; when you have to work, work; don't go to the movies." Another writes this way: "All people had to do was mention a party and I left the books."

                                        o   o   o

Eugene S. Wilson, Dean of Freshmen at Amherst College, has a very sound piece of advice. "The big job is to get students to be themselves. Most people don't dare to be a nobody; they must conform, be like everybody else. We try to tell our students that they should not be afraid to be good students—to study instead of holding a bull session."

Or, to quote Emerson: "Whoso would be a man must be a non-conformist."

VIEWPOINT

University Days
BY JAMES THURBER

I passed all the other courses that I took at my University, but I could never pass botany. This was because all botany students had to spend several hours a week in a laboratory looking through a microscope at plant cells, and I could never see through a microscope. I never once saw a cell through a microscope. This used to enrage my instructor. He would wander around the laboratory pleased with the progress all the students were making in drawing the involved and, so I am told, interesting structure of flower cells, until he came to me. I would just be standing there. "I can't see anything," I would say. He would begin patiently enough, explaining how anybody can see through a microscope, but he would always end up in a fury, claiming that I could *too* see through a microscope but just pretended that I couldn't. "It takes away from the beauty of the flowers anyway," I used to tell him. "We are not concerned solely with what I may call ⸗he *mechanics* of flars." "Well," I'd say, "I can't see anything." "Try it just once again," he'd say, and I would put my eye to the microscope and see nothing at all, except now and again a nebulous milky substance—a phenomenon of maladjustment. You were supposed to see a vivid, restless clockwork of sharply defined plant cells. "I see what looks like a lot of milk," I would tell him. This, he claimed, was the result of my not having adjusted the microscope properly, so he would readjust it for me, or rather, for himself. And I would look again and see milk.

I finally took a deferred pass, as they called it, and waited a year and tried again. (You had to pass one of the biological sciences or you couldn't graduate.) The professor had come back from vacation brown as a berry, bright-eyed, and eager to explain cell-structure again to his classes. "Well," he said to me, cheerily, when we met in the first laboratory hour of the semester, "We're going to see cells this time, aren't we?" "Yes, sir," I said. Students to right of me and to left of me and in front of me were seeing cells; what's more, they were quietly drawing pictures of them in their notebooks. Of course, I didn't see anything.

"We'll try it," the professor said to me, grimly, "with every adjustment of the microscope known to man. As God is my witness, I'll arrange this glass so that you see cells through it or I'll give up teaching. In twenty-two years of botany, I—" He cut off abruptly for he was beginning to quiver all over, like Lionel Barrymore, and he genuinely wished to hold onto his temper; his scenes with me had taken a great deal out of him.

The late James Thurber graduated from Ohio State University. He is the author of *Let Your Mind Alone, My Life and Hard Times, The Years with Ross, Thurber Country,* and *The Thurber Carnival* (New York: Harper & Row, Inc., 1945) from which this reminiscence is reprinted by permission.

So we tried it with every adjustment of the microscope known to man. With only one of them did I see anything but blackness or the familiar lacteal opacity, and that time I saw, to my pleasure and amazement, a variegated constellation of flecks, specks, and dots. These I hastily drew. The instructor, noting my activity, came back from an adjoining desk, a smile on his lips and his eyebrows high in hope. He looked at my cell drawing. "What's that?" he demanded, with a hint of a squeal in his voice. "That's what I saw," I said. "You didn't, you didn't, you didn't!" he screamed, losing control of his temper instantly, and he bent over and squinted into the microscope. His head snapped up. "That's your eye!" he shouted. "You've fixed the lens so that it reflects! You've drawn your eye!"

Another course that I didn't like, but somehow managed to pass, was economics. I went to that class straight from the botany class, which didn't help me any in understanding either subject. I used to get them mixed up. But not as mixed up as another student in my economics class who came there direct from a physics laboratory. He was a tackle on the football team, named Bolenciecwcz. At that time Ohio State University had one of the best football teams in the country, and Bolenciecwcz was one of its outstanding stars. In order to be eligible to play it was necessary for him to keep up in his studies, a very difficult matter, for while he was not dumber than an ox he was not any smarter. Most of his professors were lenient and helped him along. None gave him more hints, in answering questions, or asked him simpler ones than the economics professor,.a thin, timid man named Bassum. One day when we were on the subject of transportation and distribution, it came Bolenciecwcz's turn to answer a question. "Name one means of transportation," the professor said to him. No light came into the big tackle's eyes. "Just any means of transportation," said the professor. Bolenciecwcz sat staring at him. "That is," pursued the professor, "any medium, agency, or method of going from one place to another." Bolenciecwcz had the look of a man who is being led into a trap. "You may choose among steam, horse-drawn, or electrically propelled vehicles," said the instructor. "I might suggest the one which we commonly take in making long journeys across land." There was a profound silence in which everybody stirred uneasily, including Bolenciecwcz and Mr. Bassum. Mr. Bassum abruptly broke this silence in an amazing manner. "Choo-choo-choo," he said in a low voice, and turned instantly scarlet. He glanced appealingly around the room. All of us, of course, shared Mr. Bassum's desire that Bolenciecwcz should stay abreast of the class in economics, for the Illinois game, one of the hardest and most important of the season, was only a week off. "Toot, toot, tootoooooot!" some student with a deep voice moaned, and we all looked encouragingly at Bolenciecwcz. Somebody else gave a fine imitation of a locomotive letting off steam. Mr. Bassum himself rounded off the little show. "Ding dong, ding, dong," he said, hopefully. Bolenciecwcz was staring at the floor now, trying to think, his great brow furrowed, his huge hands rubbing together, his face red.

"How did you come to college this year, Mr. Bolenciecwcz?" asked the professor. "*Chuff*a chuffa, *chuff*a chuffa."

"M'father sent me," said the football player.

"What on?" asked Bassum.

"I git an 'lowance," said the tackle, in a low, husky voice, obviously embarrassed.

"No, no," said Bassum. "Name a means of transportation. What did you *ride* here on?"

"Train," said Bolenciecwcz.

"Quite right," said the professor. "Now, Mr. Nugent, will you tell us—"

If I went through anguish in botany and economics—for different reasons —gymnasium work was even worse. I don't even like to think about it. They wouldn't let you play games or join in the exercises with your glasses on and I couldn't see with mine off. I bumped into professors, horizontal bars, agricultural students, and swinging iron rings. Not being able to see, I could take it but I couldn't dish it out. Also, in order to pass gymnasium (and you had to pass it to graduate) you had to learn to swim if you didn't know how. I didn't like the swimming pool, I didn't like swimming, and I didn't like the swimming instructor, and after all these years I still don't. I never swam but I passed my gym work anyway, by having another student give my gymnasium number (978) and swim across the pool in my place. He was a quiet, amiable blond youth, number 473, and he would have seen through a microscope for me if we could have got away with it, but we couldn't get away with it. Another thing I didn't like about gymnasium work was that they made you strip the day you registered. It is impossible for me to be happy when I am stripped and being asked a lot of questions. Still I did better than a lanky agricultural student who was cross-examined just before I was. They asked each student what college he was in—that is, whether Arts, Engineering, Commerce, or Agriculture. "What college are you in?" the instructor snapped at the youth in front of me. "Ohio State University," he said promptly.

It wasn't that agricultural student but it was another a whole lot like him who decided to take up journalism, possibly on the ground that when farming went to hell he could fall back on newspaper work. He didn't realize, of course, that that would be very much like falling back full-length on a kit of carpenter's tools. Haskins didn't seem cut out for journalism, being too embarrassed to talk to anybody and unable to use a typewriter, but the editor of the college paper assigned him to the cow barns, the sheep house, the horse pavilion, and the animal husbandry department generally. This was a genuinely big "beat," for it took up five times as much ground and got ten times as great a legislative appropriation as the College of Liberal Arts. The agricultural student knew animals, but nevertheless his stories were dull and colorlessly written. He took all afternoon on each of them, on account of having to hunt for each letter on the typewriter. Once in a while he had to ask somebody to help him hunt. "C" and "L," in particular, were hard letters for him to find. His editor finally got pretty much annoyed at the farmer-journalist because his pieces were so uninteresting. "See here, Haskins," he snapped at him one day, "why is it we never have anything hot from you on the horse pavillion? Here we have two hundred head of horses on this campus—more than any other university in the Western Conference except Purdue—and yet you never get any real lowdown on them. Now shoot over to the horse barns and dig up something lively." Haskins shambled out and came back in about an hour; he said he had something. "Well, start it off snappily," said the editor. "Something people will read." Haskins set to work and in a couple of hours brought a sheet of typewritten paper to the desk; it was a two-hundred word story about some disease that had broken out among the horses. Its opening sentence was simple but arresting. It read: "Who has noticed the sores on the tops of the horses in the animal husbandry building?"

Ohio State was a land grant university and therefore two years of military drill was compulsory. We drilled with old Springfield rifles and studied the tactics of the Civil War even though the World War was going on at the time. At 11 o'clock each morning thousands of freshmen and sophomores used to deploy over the campus, moodily creeping up on the old chemistry building. It was good training for the kind of warfare that was waged at Shiloh but it had no connection with what was going on in Europe. Some people used to think there was German money behind it, but they didn't dare say so or they would have been thrown in jail as German spies. It was a period of muddy thought and marked, I believe, the decline of higher education in the Middle West.

PART 2

Getting Greater Returns as a Student

What Are the Basic Conditions for Effective Study?

What Are the Best Ways to Study and Prepare Assignments?

Can You Do Better on Examinations?

CHAPTER 5

What are the Basic Conditions for Effective Study?

In order to study effectively, you must have some purpose or goal. At the highest level you study simply because you want to learn something. Or perhaps, at a somewhat lower level, you study because it is the means of attaining some other goal—a better job, entrance to graduate school, prestige, glory, or to get grades that will make your parents happy. At a still lower level, a student may consider study as a necessary evil to be endured so that he can spend the remainder of his time on more enjoyable activities or to avoid having to do something even worse for him. Your goal and the intensity of your desire to achieve it determine the amount of energy you will apply to your studies, but even more important, they determine how effectively you will work, for your *attitude* toward study is every bit as important as your *aptitude*.

YOUR ATTITUDE

A good attitude toward study starts with the setting of worthwhile goals for yourself. The next step is to select the best ways of attaining them.

Any good student wants to understand his subject, whatever it is. He may also want to earn the grades generally recognized as a measure of learning. It is rare that a good student complains about having to study. He enjoys his work and has the confidence that comes from knowing that what he is now doing has led to desired results in the past. But he is always ready to improve his methods of study.

In contrast, the poorer student has poorly-conceived goals and only a hazy notion of how to proceed. He may give the impression that he just does not care. Often, the truth may be that he cares too much. He faces what seems to be an unscalable mountain with everyone standing behind him, shouting, "Let's go!" He has only a vague idea of what it is that people want from him. He has a deep feeling that even if he did understand this, he still might not be able to do it. His past experiences have frequently been filled with confusion, frustration, and failure.

> *All wish to possess knowledge but few, comparatively speaking, are willing to pay the price.*
>
> Juvenal

Because of this background he has come to hate his daily struggles. Such a student must take action immediately. He must first try to decide what he wants out of college. Then, he must assess his own strengths and weaknesses, and plan a course of action for himself. Above all, he must build up the self-confidence which comes from keeping his word to himself. This can be done by setting reasonable short-range tasks and making certain to complete them. A student with poor study habits will often promise himself that he will do much more than the average student does. He may begin to work unrealistically long hours and find the strain too great. Even if he should accomplish a heroic task once or twice, he still fails to establish consistent habits. It is better to set reasonable limits such as studying a few hours at a time. **Self-confidence is built every time a goal is met; it is weakened every time resolutions are made but not carried out.**

Neither complacent apathy nor frantic activity is an aid to effective study. What you must try to cultivate is a reasonable confidence in yourself as well as an even temper. You must also try to foster a certain amount of contentment with your lot; there are many positions in life much less pleasant than that of a college student in this country.

Ideally, your life should flow smoothly with as few unsettling interruptions as possible. By deliberate effort you can cultivate greater peace of mind. Try not to be like the distraught undergraduate who once muttered, "If I could only find some time this weekend, I would have a nervous breakdown." Directed purposes and good habits mark the difference between the successful student and the one who is always becoming unraveled.

Whether your past experiences have been gratifying or otherwise, the obligation to study now is, in the final analysis, yours alone. No one can possibly force you, and the amount of help anyone—your instructors, your parents, your friends, or even this book—can give is very limited. When the tumult and the shouting die, it is just you and the printed page.

To summarize, you can help yourself by first developing the best possible attitude and then finding the best methods and techniques for studying—those which work for you. Following such practices will not only save you time and effort, but will also help make college the enjoyable and rewarding experience it should be.

YOUR CONDITIONS FOR STUDYING

I expected college to be easy, with no worry about subjects. But I found that in order to pass you have to study, and study hard. I'm not disappointed because I have to study, but because you have to study more outside of class than in class.

College Freshman

Over the years a good many recommendations have been made as to the best way to study. Some are based on psychological research, some on the experience of the individual writer, some on folklore or superstition. Some methods will be valid for you; others will not. The important point to remember in considering these suggestions is that none of them is of any value unless it works for you.

Improving concentration

When students are asked to describe difficulties they have in studying, they most often say that they cannot keep their minds on their work. Study periods then become internal struggles between the need to study and the inability to concentrate. As a result, such students are easily bothered or distracted and, even worse, they become so tired that they cannot do their best. As Virginia Voeks has commented:

> ... Inability to concentrate is rendered yet more distressing by the fatigue which accompanies it. . . . Poor concentration leads to fatigue. Fatigue leads to poor concentration.
>
> Both poor concentration and fatigue are caused in large part by conflict. We try to study, but simultaneously we are half set to abandon the whole business and do something else. . . . We debate going out for the evening. We try to figure out some personal problems. We do all these things and simultaneously we try to study. . . . As a consequence we become tired. . . . Fatigue always results when we tear against ourselves (1).

Quiet is generally regarded as a necessary condition for concentration, but some individuals can do well in noisy surroundings and some can do even better. Clearly, external stimuli are not the main causes of distraction for many people. More important is the state of mind and degree of concentration of the student himself. Some can be distracted by a whisper; some cannot by a sonic boom or even a younger sister.

Concentration can be improved if you reduce distractions within you, by reminding yourself of your goals. Some students suggest that you write down any nagging problems or obligations, so that you can stop thinking about them for the present. The most insidious of distractions are the competing attractions.

Try to set out a reasonable amount of work for yourself within the time you have, instead of being overwhelmed by the enormity of the entire course that lies ahead.

Take short rest periods; say, ten minutes or so during which you do something quite different, such as one of the tasks you have written down. Other suggestions for reducing distractions and increasing concentration will be found in the next chapter.

Where to study

One of the most common suggestions, and one that many students report as very helpful, is to have one particular place in which to study, such as a desk in the student's room. This place is not used for any other purpose. Loafing, daydreaming, or recreational reading are done elsewhere. Such students consciously try to train themselves to study whenever they are in this particular place. Frequently, the college library is recommended as a good place for study, but only a minority of students follow this advice. Yet there is evidence that studying in the library is actually helpful. In one investigation each student was matched with another student according to academic abilities. One member of each pair was then assigned to study in the library while the other student studied elsewhere. Results showed that the students who studied in the library did better than those who did not. If your college has more than one library or study room you may find it helpful to use one which is not used by your friends, who —splendid as they no doubt are—may distract you from your work. Some students make a practice of finding empty classrooms for lone studying and report that this works well for them. Others use a public library if they can find one which is sufficiently quiet.

Some individuals can study almost anywhere: on a crowded bus or train, on the campus or in a park facing a busy street, even in a restaurant or theater lobby. Some fortunate ones can study while working as night clerks or as switchboard operators. However, before trying any of these more exotic settings, it would seem best to try studying where most successful students do: in one obviously suitable place such as the library or your own room.

Wherever you study, it is essential that you have adequate *light* which falls uniformly over the entire page and does not cause glare in your eyes. It is better to have indirect lighting which illuminates the entire area rather than a spot-beam directly on the page. There should be more than one light in the room. Some students prefer the cool fluorescent tubes while others favor incandescent bulbs; some like to switch from one to the other. It is worthwhile to get the light you find most pleasant.

Besides adequate light, a suitable place to study should have proper *temperature* and *humidity*. Even if you are not aware of these, they can affect your efficiency. Most people do their best work when the room temperature is near 68 degrees and the relative humidity is about 40 per cent.

Your furniture

It is generally believed that holding your body erect and alert has a beneficial effect on the vitality of your mind. For this reason, it is often suggested that a student does better when sitting in a straight-backed arm-chair which is comfortable, but not too comfortable.

The condition of your desk may also affect your efficiency. Many students permit their desks to become so cluttered that the amount of work space is severely restricted. One solution to this problem would be to keep buying new desks as the old ones become completely buried. If this is not feasible, you may wish merely to inspect your present desk critically and then get rid of all the useless material which has accumulated.

While inspecting your desk you might also consider whether it is in the best possible position to shield you from certain avoidable distractions. It is usually better not to face a window. It is also better not to face your roommate if you wish to avoid time-wasting talk when you have an assignment to prepare.

Avoiding other distractions

Any influence that diverts your attention is bound to reduce your efficiency. For most college students the most distracting influence is their *friends*—friends who drop in; friends who telephone; friends who just want to talk; friends with exciting plans for the evening; friends who have already done their own studying; or friends who do not expect to pass their own courses anyway. Now friendship is, of course, one of the greatest things in the world, but to be a successful student you must develop the moral stamina to resist the demands of friendship when they come at the wrong time. Remember, the friendly people who appear at college alumni reunions are almost invariably those who studied enough to graduate with their class.

Another source of distraction is the student's *relatives,* who, with the best motives in the world, manage to take him away from his studies. There is only one known remedy for this. If you live at home, and if for any reason you find that you cannot study effectively there, you must arrange your schedule so that your college work is done elsewhere.

Still another of the good things in life that can deter you from studying is *love.* Ignoring the cynical viewpoint that the only sure cure for love is marriage, let us consider some of the suggestions that have been made by Bowman for studying while you are away from the love of your life (2). First, place the picture of your loved one where you cannot see it from your desk. One look can set off a whole chain of thoughts, and there goes another evening. Second, do not reread letters just before studying; and as for writing letters, determine for yourself whether you study better by writing early in the day or later. Third, do not interrupt your reading to dream for "just a minute." It is difficult to return to work. Fourth, try working to please your loved one, to make yourself someone to be proud of. Rarely does anyone brag about a betrothed who did poorly in college because of a lack of emotional control.

Whether you study better with music playing is a matter for you to decide. Some students report they like to have a radio playing, particularly an FM "all-music" station. They believe that they are forced to shut out the sound and that this in turn forces them to concentrate better. Such forcing of concentration can only be done at the cost of some expenditure of energy, but these students apparently pay the cost willingly. Cole and Ferguson (3) suggest that many students today are so unused to silence and isolation that they actually require the noise and "companionship" provided by a radio playing softly. As for television, there is no question that it makes effective studying impossible.

Rituals and fetishes

A number of students confide that certain peculiar routines and practices are helpful to them. Some like to pile all the books they will need for the evening on the right side of the desk, and as they finish with each, they pile it on the left side. As the evening progresses they can enjoy watching one stack diminish as the other grows. Some students seem to feel more comfortable in the presence of their souvenirs and trophies.

There are still other strange rituals and fetishes that students use to keep themselves in an appropriate frame of mind for studying. We will not list them here for fear of adding to the world's burden of odd behaviors; but if you study better while eating crackers, or wearing an old sweatshirt, and if such practices are not harmful to yourself or distracting to others, by all means use them. As we have said before, it is up to you to **follow the suggestions that work for you.**

YOUR USE OF TIME

Perhaps the most valuable result of all education is the ability to make yourself do the thing you have to do, when it ought to be done, whether you like it or not. . . . However early a man's training begins, it is probably the last lesson that he learns thoroughly.
                                                                                    T. H. Huxley

Why you should prepare a time schedule

College students are surrounded by activities competing for their attention and time. It is impossible to do everything, yet many students have the idea that any form of scheduling or time planning is a menace to their personal liberty. On the contrary, scheduling is essential to effectiveness. It can help you gain the truest form of personal freedom, the mastery of one's own affairs. It does not mean becoming a slave to time. Scheduling results in the liberation of time: time for relaxation, time for social activities, time for the things which make life enjoyable. Scheduling your time can free you from uncertainty, guilt, and fear of the future.

Schedules sometimes have to be broken, but that should be no cause for discouragement or worry; no plan should be more rigid than necessary. Apollodorus tells us that Procrustes had an iron bed to which he tied his victims. If they were too short he stretched them, and if they were too tall, he cut off their legs to fit the bed. Avoid making your schedule such a bed and yourself the hapless victim tied to it.

How to plan your schedule

Scheduling itself requires planning. An arbitrary timetable is apt to be little better than useless. It is not enough simply to divide the day into hourly or half-hourly periods and assign some activity to each. You must take into account what you want to do as well as what you have to do.

Do not make the common freshman mistake of underestimating how much time will be needed for classes and study. You may be scheduled for only fifteen class hours per week, but you will generally have to study *at least two hours* for each class hour and you may need to spend additional time in the laboratory and in physical education classes. You will have to spend more time on some courses than others. Be prepared to modify your schedule as you learn more about how much time each course demands of you.

Time is also required for purposes other than studying and going to class—you have to sleep, eat, bathe, dress, exercise, do personal chores, and participate in social activities. With all this, it is to your benefit to leave some *unscheduled time* in which you may simply breathe, look into space, or chew a blade of grass.

Your primary concern in scheduling is not how much time you have for study, but how well you use the twenty-four hours in a day. You want to make the best possible use of each one. Therefore, you will want, first, to analyze how you are using your time, now, and second, to rearrange your activities so that you can achieve order and economy.

You will need three forms to plan your schedule (see tables at end of this chapter).

Activity inventory

Upon this sheet (Form A), for one typical week, keep a careful record of how you spend each thirty minutes of your time. Be specific. Be sure you do not overlook routine activities, scholarly activities, recreational or extracurricular activities. Be honest with yourself. If you spend half an hour at a campus hangout, indicate it. When you are through with your activity inventory, you should have accounted for 168 hours.

Activity analysis

Now group the activities which you have recorded chronologically into logical categories on Form B. Add up the amount of time spent on each activity. Examine the results carefully. You will probably decide you have spent too much time on some activities and too little on others. In the last column write down the adjustments you think you ought to make.

Time schedule

Form C may not be practicable for every student but, in any event, it should be examined for suggestions. Some students will prefer to make up a regular weekly schedule based upon Forms A and B; others may choose to vary their schedule from week to week as conditions change. Certain students may find it valuable to break down general activities covering weeks or months into specific daily tasks. Any schedule should avoid rigidity, overloading with similar activities in succession, and unwise distribution of study or practice sessions. As a rule, you should not schedule less than 7 or 8 hours each night for sleep and not less than 24 to 30 hours a week for study if you are carrying 12 to 15 hours of classwork.

YOUR PHYSICAL HEALTH

Get enough sleep

There is a well-recognized vicious "circle of fatigue" often seen in students. The cycle works in this way:

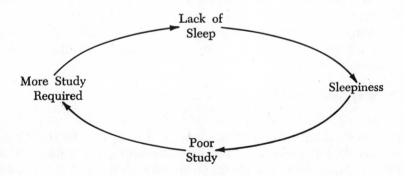

Obviously, the place to break up this cycle is at the point of lack of sleep. If you find that you are often sleepy during the day although your general health is satisfactory, it is likely that you are not getting enough sleep. Remember that the amount of sleep you require is a thoroughly individual matter which you must determine. The average requirement is said to be between seven and eight hours a night; but for some people this is not enough, while for others, it may be more than sufficient. Some individuals believe they can get along with a slight deficit in sleep all week if they have one morning during which they can sleep late. Others find that such a routine simply does not work for them. Only your own experience can answer the question of how much sleep you need.

> I forget who it was that recommended men for their soul's good to do each day two things they disliked. . . . It is a precept that I have followed scrupulously; for every day I have got up and I have gone to bed.
>
> **Somerset Maugham**

Some basic research on sleep by Nathaniel Kleitman (4) may be of value to you in understanding the problems involved. Dr. Kleitman found that a person's temperature fluctuates during a twenty-four hour period. When he sleeps his temperature drops. That is why someone napping on a couch may need a light blanket, although if he were lying down but awake, he would feel comfortable without extra covering. When a person's temperature is at its high point for the day, he feels alert and active. When it falls, he feels sleepy or "dopey." A majority of individuals naturally have their high point in the morning. These "early birds" like to rise early, may need no alarm clock, generally eat a hearty breakfast, and sail into their work with zest. By nine or ten o'clock at night, however, they begin to droop and to think longingly of bed. If they have to study overtime, they prefer to get up early for this purpose. Others, the "night owls," reach a temperature peak later in the day. They must be awakened in the morning, hate to get up, shudder at breakfast, and approach their work with reluctance. By late afternoon, however, they are operating with efficiency and they prefer to stay up late at night to study. Although these patterns are seemingly built-in, their intensity varies from person to person, and Kleitman believes that they can usually be successfully altered, particularly by younger people.

You can draw certain implications from this research for your own use. Try to work with your own pattern if convenient and if possible.

Study the subject which is hardest for you at the time when you are at your best, saving easier subjects for your low-efficiency times. But always remember that the human organism has been able to survive because it is adaptable. You must try to strike some balance between your own needs and the demands of society as represented by your college and your associates.

Eat properly

In order to function at your best, you must eat properly. Your body requires adequate amounts of calories, proteins, fats, carbohydrates, minerals, vitamins, water, and roughage.

Occasionally one finds students impairing their effectiveness by trying bizarre and faddish diets. Anyone who wishes to reduce his weight should cut down on the *quantity* of food he eats, particularly the quantity of carbohydrates found abundantly in most desserts.

College students sometimes attempt to subsist on hamburgers and colas, which may represent foods they were denied while under stronger parental control, but which are inadequate to furnish an adult's nutritional requirements. For good health everyone should eat adequately, but avoid overeating.

> **Plenus venter non studet libentur. (A full belly does not study willingly.)**
>
> **Latin proverb, quoted by H. L. Mencken**

Recreation

A certain amount of recreation is both desirable and necessary for everyone. No one can do well with his nose to the grindstone for too long a period of time. At least one or two evenings a week should be devoted to some activity not connected with your academic work.

Stimulants

One of the most harmful things that some students do to themselves is to attempt to improve their performance by using stimulants, such as large quantities of coffee or even so-called "pep" pills. These can be effective only for very short periods of time and are invariably followed by a *reaction* of extreme fatigue and confusion. For a student who has kept himself awake all night before an examination, the reaction usually comes just as the examination itself begins. Consequently, he is at his worst when he should be at his best. Whatever benefits he may have derived from the last-minute cramming are lost in his inability to express himself even on topics that he knows perfectly well.

That alcohol in any form can be used as a stimulant is a persistent bit of American folklore. Actually, alcohol acts as a depressant, particularly where a person's ability to judge his own actions is concerned. Sometimes people have the illusion that they do better work with the aid of alcohol. Repeated experiments have shown that they merely become unable to tell how badly they are doing. Stimulants or pseudo-stimulants have no place in effective studying.

NOTES TO CHAPTER 5

(1) Virginia Voeks, *On Becoming an Educated Person* (Philadelphia, Pennsylvania: W. B. Saunders Company, 1964), pp. 109-110.

(2) Henry A. Bowman, *Marriage for Moderns* (New York: McGraw-Hill Book Co., 1942), pp. 42-43.

(3) Luella Cole and Jessie Mary Ferguson, *Student's Guide to Effective Study* (New York: Holt, Rinehart & Winston, Inc., 1956), p. 19. See also: C. Bird and D. M. Bird, *Learning More by Effective Study* (New York: Appleton-Century-Crofts, 1945.)

(4) Nathaniel Kleitman, *Sleep and Wakefulness* (rev. ed.) (Chicago: University of Chicago Press, 1963).

SUGGESTIONS FOR FURTHER READING

Chandler, Elliott H., *The Effective Student*. New York: Harper and Row, 1966.

Ehrlich, Eugene H., *How to Study Better and Get Higher Marks*. New York: Thomas Y. Crowell Company, 1961.

Gilbert, Doris W., *Study in Depth*. New York: Prentice-Hall, Inc., 1966.

Pauk, Walter, *How to Study in College*. Boston: Houghton Mifflin Co., 1962.

Robinson, F. F., *Effective Study* (rev. ed.). New York: Harper and Row, 1962.

Staton, Thomas F., *R.S.V.P. . . . a Dynamic Approach to Study*. Chicago: Scott, Foresman and Company, 1966.

Tussing, Lyle, *Study and Succeed*. New York: John Wiley and Sons, Inc., 1963.

Table 1

Form A

ACTIVITY INVENTORY

A.M.	Mon.	Tues.	Wed.	Thurs.	Fri.	Sat.	Sun.	P.M.	Mon.	Tues.	Wed.	Thurs.	Fri.	Sat.	Sun.
12:00								12:00							
12:30								12:30							
1:00								1:00							
1:30								1:30							
2:00								2:00							
2:30								2:30							
3:00								3:00							
3:30								3:30							
4:00								4:00							
4:30								4:30							
5:00								5:00							
5:30								5:30							
6:00								6:00							
6:30								6:30							
7:00								7:00							
7:30								7:30							
8:00								8:00							
8:30								8:30							
9:00								9:00							
9:30								9:30							
10:00								10:00							
10:30								10:30							
11:00								11:00							
11:30								11:30							

Table 2

ACTIVITY ANALYSIS

Form B

ITEM	Monday		Tuesday		Wednesday		Thursday		Friday		Saturday		Sunday		Total	Adjustments	
	Time	Amt.	Time	Amt.	Time	Amt.	Time	Amt.	Time	Amt.	Time	Amt.	Time	Amt.	Amt.	+	−
Sleeping																	
Dressing, Washing																	
Eating																	
Travelling																	
School—Class 1																	
" " 2																	
" " 3																	
" " 4																	
" " 5																	
" " 6																	
Study—Subject 1																	
" " 2																	
" " 3																	
" " 4																	
" " 5																	
" " 6																	
Extracurricular																	
Outside Work																	
Recreation																	
Exercise																	
Social Activities																	
Home Chores																	
Amusement																	
Religion																	
Reading																	
Resting																	
Other																	
TOTALS																	

103

Table 3

Form C

TIME SCHEDULE

Time*	Monday	Tuesday	Wednesday	Thursday	Friday	Saturday	Sunday

* Be sure to account for a full twenty-four (24) hours. Rule off a horizontal line after each activity.

CHAPTER 6

What are the Best Ways to Study and Prepare Assignments?

YOUR METHOD OF STUDYING READINGS

Many suggestions have been made as to the most helpful methods for students to use in studying their reading assignments. The best of these suggestions are based on the findings of the educational psychologists, who have amassed considerable data on comprehension and forgetting. Many of them recommend that the study of a text follow five distinct stages or steps (1). These five steps can be remembered conveniently in this acrostic based on the word, STUDY:

S— SURVEY the entire assignment
T—THINK of questions
U—UNDERSTAND your reading
D—DEMONSTRATE your understanding
Y— YOU REVIEW the entire assignment

Step One—SURVEY

Begin by surveying the chapter or section you are about to study, concentrating first on its *title*. What could be written on this subject? What do you already know about it and what would you like to learn?

Next read the headings of the sub-sections, preferably in the table of contents, and think about each sub-heading there as you have thought about the main heading.

Then turn to the assignment itself and scan the first paragraph or two to see if the author explains how the chapter is organized. If he has done so, these paragraphs should be read again more carefully.

Next read the section headings for the rest of the chapter and a sentence or two in each paragraph. Also read the captions of all illus-

---

Study is like the heaven's glorious sun, that will not be deepsearch'd with saucy looks. . . .

Shakespeare

---

trations and graphs. Make use of the different type sizes and faces employed by the author to show how the text is organized.

Then, if there is a summary at the end of the section, read it through slowly and carefully.

Finally, read any questions or problems at the end of the chapter. Ordinarily, this entire survey of the assignment should not take more than ten or fifteen minutes; only five may be sufficient.

The art of reading implies the art of non-reading and more energy is sometimes needed in order to skip rather than to continue useless drifting. Many would-be scholars never learn anything, not only because they cannot read, but also because they cannot stop reading.

George Sarton

107

Step Two—THINK OF QUESTIONS

Having a question in mind when you read is one of the most effective means of learning and retaining subject matter. Always try to anticipate questions which might be asked about the reading. What? Why? Who? Where? When? How? You may also wish to ask, what does this mean to me? Does this match my own experiences or beliefs? How good is the author's evidence for his assertions? You may wish to write out such questions or you may merely ask them of yourself mentally. If you have a workbook which contains questions you will want to make use of them also. Some of the questions you construct or find may turn out to be the very questions asked on an examination.

Socrates recognized the value of the question more than two thousand years ago: he always began with a question, not an answer. In modern times, Dewey has also emphasized that questions lead to new knowledge. Once an answer is accepted, he said, the process of learning tends to stop.

Step Three—UNDERSTAND YOUR READING

After completing the two preliminary steps—surveying the entire section and thinking of questions—you are ready to start your intensive reading. Many students find that it helps to underline and otherwise mark up their textbooks at this time. This may make the book difficult to re-sell, but its main purpose is to serve you as a tool, not a trade-in. Some students prefer to take notes based on the text or even to outline entire sections. Taking notes from a text is much simpler than taking notes from a speaker, although the general procedure is similar. If you decide to underline or mark the book, several suggestions are in order. First, do not make any marks until you have carefully read an entire section or at least several paragraphs. Until you have done so, you will not understand the relationship of the ideas. Then go back and underline only the most important points, and next, the most important details or examples of those points. Details or examples may be numbered. Some students, particularly those in law schools, prefer to use colored pencils for underlining and annotating their texts and notes. Major points are marked in red, minor ones in blue, examples in green, and so on.

A brief title describing the contents of the paragraph may be written in the margin; or better still, a question answered by the paragraph may be written there. When studying exceptionally difficult material such as a philosophical treatise which lacks the headings found in most textbooks, a useful technique is to draw a diagonal line in the margin and characterize with a word or two the function which the paragraph serves in the argument. Below the diagonal write another word or two which summarizes the entire content of the paragraph. These marginal notes then act as landmarks so that you can easily reorient yourself if you become lost.

Be perfectly certain that you **understand every single word** in your reading assignment. When you find an unfamiliar term, try to guess its meaning from the context or from its structure. Then see how well you guessed by finding the term in a dictionary, or in the glossary, if your book has one. If your book has no glossary, you can start your own by listing the unfamiliar term in your notebook, following it with either a brief definition or a reference to where the definition can be found. Be particularly alert for familiar words which are used in a restricted or special sense in your subject. For example, the words *seed* and *animal* have definitions in biology which are significantly different from their meanings in daily life. Pay particular attention to illustrations, graphs, charts, maps, and similar material. In a well-written text, these have been carefully chosen to make important points and are very effective in helping you learn.

As part of your routine you should also prepare the materials you will use for later review, such as lists of terms with definitions, tables of dates, and collections of key formulas.

This stage of your study procedure—studying for understanding—is by far the most time-consuming, and you must be prepared to spend all the time that you require to master the material, even if it means re-reading the passage many times. What counts is not how many times you read the chapter but rather how much you get out of it.

Some students try to read everything at the same rate of speed. Your speed should vary with your purpose and with the nature of the material. When you survey new material and when you review the old, you should try to scan rapidly. When you study for deeper understanding you should read as slowly as necessary. **Try to read at an appropriate rate.**

Step Four—DEMONSTRATE YOUR UNDERSTANDING

The simplest and quickest way of demonstrating your understanding of the reading is to turn back to the table of contents and repeat Step Two. That is, you again think of *questions* for each heading in the table. If you can ask and answer good questions with reasonable ease, you are justified in feeling that you have begun to understand the reading. If, at first, you cannot answer your own questions based on the table of contents, it is simple to turn back to the text and study the section again. You may have to do this several times.

A more thorough and generally more satisfactory way of demonstrating understanding is to write out your questions and **practice writing clear, brief, and accurate answers.** This procedure, laborious though it may be, is absolutely necessary for students who have not had enough experience in taking essay examinations. Students who are confident of their ability to write well under the pressures of an examination may not have to write out complete answers but may find it sufficient to indicate their responses with a brief outline or even a few phrases.

Another way of demonstrating your understanding, and the way which is sometimes the most fun, is to get together with others in your class and practice asking each other questions. The success of this method depends on the persons with whom you choose to study. If the others are even more serious than you are about studying, you may find group studying helpful, provided that you have done your own preliminary reading thoroughly enough. Often, however, group study sessions among college students get off the track very quickly and the result may be a social success but an academic failure.

Step Five—YOU REVIEW

The final step is for you to reread the text slowly and carefully, preferably more than once. If you find that what you are reading is now completely familiar, so much the better. What you are doing at this time is sometimes called "overlearning," which psychologists have shown to be a valuable learning technique.

If, on the other hand, you still do not understand some part of the text, first mark the passage. Then try to approach it in a different way instead of merely repeating what you have been doing. Ask yourself, what is this writer trying to tell me? Why can't I understand him? Try to restate his words. Try to imagine the negative or the converse of his statement. If your writer mentions any quantities, try to give a simple numerical example. You can also analyze a passage sentence by sentence, and perhaps overcome your difficulties one at a time.

As an example, let us try some of these techniques on this somewhat cryptic sentence from a physical geography text: *"Variability of precipitation commonly increases directly with aridity."*

1) **What is the writer trying to tell me?** "He's apparently trying to tell me something about rainfall."
2) **What is keeping me from understanding him?** "I don't know what he means by "variability . . . increases directly with . . .""

3) **How can I restate this?** "The drier it is, the more variable the rainfall."
4) **What is the opposite?** "The drier it is, the more regular the rainfall." (That doesn't seem right!)
5) **What is the converse?** "The wetter it is, the more constant the rainfall."
6) **What is a numerical example?** Let's take a 1″ rainfall in a desert where there usually are only 2″ a year. If more rain doesn't come, we have lost half of the year's supply. But if 1″ doesn't fall in a jungle, where there are 100″ per year, we have only lost 1%. So, *the drier it is in an area the more difference a little rain can make.*

PREPARING YOUR WRITTEN ASSIGNMENTS

Tell them they won't get by in college if they don't do their home work!
                                                      College Instructor

The essential first step in preparing any assignment is to make sure you understand exactly what it is that you are supposed to do. Every assignment, no matter how simple it sounds, should be written on your calendar as a matter of course. If you are uncertain about any of the details, clear up your questions before you leave the classroom. In this way, you can avoid having to figure out whom to call at eleven o'clock at night to find out whether you were supposed to do "the even-numbered problems except number 10," or "the odd-numbered problems plus number 10." Assignments given in class should always be regarded as your *minimum* obligations. The instructor may have assigned only half of the problems at the end of a chapter, but if you have completed those and still are not sure that you understand the techniques involved, nothing prevents you from doing additional problems until you do understand.

When to do your assignments

Written assignments must be submitted to the instructor at the time they are due. The only way you can be certain to accomplish this is by preparing them ahead of time, preferably soon after the assignment is made, for it is at this time that the instructor's explanations are best remembered. If you wait until just before the due date, you may lose out in two ways. First, you will have to start by laboriously relearning something that you may have understood clearly at one time. Second, you run the risk of having something turn up on that final crucial night which might make it impossible for you to do the assignment as you had planned. Some students ask their instructors for extensions of time for assignments. This not only embarrasses the instructor who has troubles of his own, but also reveals a lack of foresight and self-discipline on the part of the student. The solution is simple. Do your assignments at once, and get them off your conscience. An army administrative officer was once asked how he explained his rapid rise in rank. He replied, "To tell you the truth, my secret is that I hate work. I just can't stand to have it around, so I do it and get rid of it!"

Form of assignments

Every written assignment deserves to be written in the correct form, following the particular college's customs in such matters as where you write your name and other identifying information. Assignments should bear the date they are due, not the date they are prepared.

If it is at all possible, your assignments should be typed. If you cannot get them typed, pay particular attention to the legibility of your handwriting. Whether your instructor mentions it or not, **neatness does count.** He is predisposed to admire what is attractive and to suspect that what looks bad, is bad.

WRITING A REFERENCE PAPER

Writing a reference paper or a long theme will be one of the most important activities you will undertake in college. Several such papers are required in most freshman composition or rhetoric courses; many of your advanced courses all the way through college require them; and finally, the writing of a long original paper turns out to be the most imposing requirement for the highest academic degree. Obviously, the skills you acquire while learning to write—how to gather information, evaluate it, and present it in an effective manner—are essential for getting through college. Even more important, finding accurate information and then applying it to the solution of a problem is fundamental to most occupations after you leave college. Engineers, doctors, salesmen, clergymen, lawyers, teachers, administrators, all are required to express themselves accurately and effectively in writing.

The skills involved are basically the same whether you are writing a single paper or an entire book. We can divide the process of writing a reference paper into six steps:

1) Choosing a topic   4) Writing
2) Gathering notes   5) Revising
3) Organizing the paper   6) Preparing the final copy

Choosing a topic

The choosing of a topic is often as difficult and challenging as the actual writing, yet careful consideration at this stage is indispensable for a successful paper. Occasionally, an instructor will assign a definite topic. More often, he will furnish a list of suggestions, or he may ask you to find your own. There are many sources for such topics.

Your interests

It is often recommended that you choose a topic in which you have an immediate interest. Your hobby or favorite sport, a person who interests you, the occupation you plan to enter, a question which is troubling you—all these offer possibilities that may be explored. Other suitable topics for research may be suggested by your working experiences or travels.

Your textbook

Your instructor may prefer a more scholarly subject for your paper. If so, you can find a virtually unlimited source of topics in your textbook, which usually is a survey of a broad field of knowledge. Thus, many ideas which are interesting or important are covered only briefly in the text and are therefore good subjects for further study. Also, you are likely to find bibliographical references in your text which are a good starting point for finding further material. If you use the text for this purpose, be sure to bring the references up to date by consulting the *Readers' Guide to Periodical Literature* and other similar indexes. This is always necessary because there is often a considerable lag between the time a new discovery is first reported and when it appears in the texts.

Class discussions

Another source of topics for term papers is found right in class where discussions frequently turn up interesting questions for students who are alert and receptive.

Applying one interest to another

Some excellent term papers have been written by combining one interest with another; for example, "The Psychology of the Baseball

Fan," "The Economic Impact of Foreign Cars on the American Market," and "Actresses as Ego-Ideals of Adolescents."

Topics to avoid

There are four common faults to guard against when choosing a subject for a paper. Avoid topics that are too trite, too broad, too narrow, or too charged with emotion. Topics that are *trite* and *overworked* become dull not only for the reader but also for you as the writer. The very fact that a topic has been productive for other students in the past may be an indication that you should choose something else.

Avoid topics which are *too broad* for adequate treatment in your theme. Papers on such topics become so superficial or so incomplete as to be of little value to anyone. It is, however, a sound approach to begin by choosing a more general subject, doing some extensive reading, and then narrowing it down to a size you can handle. For example, you may be interested in the life of Napoleon, but obviously this is too broad a topic for a term paper. Confining your topic to his early education might be more suitable. If you were writing in the field of chemistry, the subject, "Modern Plastics," would be far too broad for any term paper, but the story of one particular plastic might be manageable.

Shun topics which are so *narrow* or *obscure* that it is impossible to find enough information about them. New research reported in the popular press often has this limitation. The solution to this problem is either to broaden the scope of your paper or to abandon the topic and choose another.

Finally, it is best to avoid choosing any topic about which you cannot be cool, detached, and objective. *Wild enthusiasm, bitter antagonism, and fulsome admiration* tend to result in term papers which are over-written and unacceptable.

Your instructor stands ready to help you avoid mistakes in choosing a subject for your term paper. From experience, he knows how to recognize topics which are too threadbare, too general, too specific, or too emotion-laden. He can also help you to clarify and delimit a topic and can often suggest sources of information which may not occur to you. In short, you can save time and effort by getting the help of your instructor *before* you have made major mistakes.

Gathering notes

In gathering the notes or material for the paper, you will need to use all the resources of the library as they are explained in Chapter 8.

Your notes should be taken on index cards, 3″ x 5″ or 4″ x 6″ or 5″ x 8″ depending upon your own preference. (You may use slips of paper instead of cards. Paper is less expensive.) You will need three kinds of cards: "bibliography," "note," and "idea." Each of the three kinds may be a different size or color if you wish.

The first step is to prepare your *bibliography cards*, each of which will contain complete information on a single reference source for your paper. This source may be a book, a magazine article, an encyclopedia, or perhaps an unpublished reference, such as a letter or report of an interview. It will save time if you accustom yourself to writing the reference in the form which you are required to use in the final copy of your paper. When you make use of many references it is helpful to write comments on the bibliography cards. These remarks may include relevant chapter headings, or your opinion as to the material's particular usefulness. You should also **record the library call number** of your reference and perhaps where you learned about it. These cards are strictly for your own eyes; use them for preserving any information you may need later. When you finally come to type the bibliography for your term paper, all you will have to do is alphabetize the bibliography cards and you are ready to start.

The second type of card needed is the *note card*. This will contain information that you have extracted from the reference sources. The most important rule to follow in preparing your note cards is to **write only one point on a card.** The second rule is to **cite the exact source of the point** briefly but accurately. (Some writers number their bibliography cards and then use the same number to identify their note cards. Others identify their note cards with the last name of the author. Whichever practice you follow, always **give the exact page** of the source. This is necessary for writing footnotes, and useful in case you want to verify the point for yourself later.)

Each card should also have a *brief title* or label at the top, describing its subject matter. Write on only one side of a card and use ink. According to Cole and Ferguson, (2) you will probably need 100 to 200 cards or "note slips" for a 15 to 20 page term paper.

Ordinarily, the information you write on your note card will be in the form of a paraphrase or summary of the writer's words. You may, however, wish to use a direct quotation occasionally for emphasis or for precise accuracy. Be sure to **use quotation marks** around any excerpts from a written passage, and thus avoid the possibility of *plagiarism*, a term which will be explained later in this chapter.

In taking notes, it is essential to discriminate between fact and opinion, and between established principles and speculative guessing. Your paper will be more interesting and more complete if you are alert to instances where different authorities either agree or disagree. Greater weight should of course be given to authors who cite the evidence for their conclusions rather than those who merely make dogmatic assertions. By the same token, when writing your own paper, always back your opinions with data. James Boyce wrote: "It is Facts that are needed; Facts, Facts, Facts. When facts have been supplied, each of us can try to reason from them."

Idea cards are similar to note cards except that they record your own original thoughts or questions on the subject rather than the thoughts of another writer. It is best to get your valuable ideas into writing promptly before you lose them. Putting them on cards will make it easier to fit them into the paper later on. In order to distinguish between your own ideas and those of others, it is best to **sign** idea cards with your initials. Otherwise, you may later confuse them with note cards for which you have neglected to record a source.

Organizing the paper

As soon as possible, you should prepare a preliminary outline for the entire paper. There are two ways of doing this: deductively and inductively. If you are writing on a topic with which you are already reasonably familiar, you can proceed *deductively* by making your tentative outline before you begin taking notes. If, on the other hand, you know very little about your topic, you must proceed *inductively* by first gathering a quantity of notes and then organizing them into logical categories, making use of the labels on your cards. In either procedure, you should revise your outline continually as new information becomes available to you.

When preparing an outline for a reference paper it is essential to **have a general plan** in mind. This may be as simple as the plan of one gifted backwoods preacher who explained the success of his sermons as follows: "First, I tell 'em what I'm goin' to tell 'em. Then I tell 'em. Then I tell 'em what I told 'em." In other words, his sermons all had a beginning, a middle, and an end; or, if you prefer, an introduction, a body or text, and a conclusion. You may organize your paper in this way or you may wish to use some other general plan of organization. One of the following four plans may be chosen: *time, two-phase, three-phase,* or *stage-by-stage.*

Organization by time is useful for some historical papers. It consists of dividing a **longer period of time**—that is, the entire scope of the paper—into **shorter sub-periods of time** and devoting a section of the paper to each sub-period. For example, the political history of Czechoslovakia can be usefully divided into five periods: 1526-1918, 1918-1939,

1939-1945, 1946-1968, 1968-. How well this method works depends upon the standards used for determining the beginning or end of a period.

Organization in two phases means that your paper is divided into two major parts. In the first part, a question is asked or a problem is posed in detail. In the second part, an answer or a solution is set forth. (This method of organization is sometimes called Platonic dialogue or dialectic.)

Organization in three phases involves three major divisions for your paper:

1) *Thesis*, in which a situation evolves or a problem is set forth;
2) *Antithesis*, in which opposition develops to the first situation or suggested solutions to the problem are proposed;
3) *Synthesis*, in which the problem is resolved for the time being. (This method is called Hegelian dialectic.)

Still another method of organization is to start with introductory or preliminary material and then advance **stage by stage to a climax** which consists of your final and most important point. Of course, there are other ways to organize a paper. Some of these ways can be found by examining the table of contents of a good book on your topic or a related topic.

After you have constructed a general outline for your paper, pick out the major ideas which will be the cores of your paragraphs. Decide how emphasis requires you to place these ideas. At this time you should tentatively choose your topic sentence for each paragraph. Then develop your ideas. What you should seek is not an abstract of the work of others but a *creation* of your own—the difference between some tubes of paint and a scrap of canvas on one hand and a finished painting on the other: or, to use another metaphor, the difference between an array of ingredients on the kitchen table and a cake ready for eating.

Much of your creative work may come in the form of new comparisons or new contrasts, simplified analyses of complicated issues, or new examples which illustrate and illuminate general principles. Keep in mind that one of the main benefits you should get from college is an increased ability to think creatively. The reference paper is one effective way to strengthen this ability.

After you have written a complete sentence outline and are reasonably well-satisfied with it, put it away for a day or two, and then re-examine it to see if it still seems to make sense to you. At this time your final revision of the outline should be made and conventional symbols assigned to each point. Then take your note cards and idea cards and mark each one with the appropriate outline symbol. Once you have sorted your cards by symbol and have discarded any duplicate cards, you are ready to write your paper.

Writing

Begin writing. Follow your outline but **let the writing flow:** your self-questioning is over. You know what you want to say. **Say it!** Choose words which are appropriate to your subject; vary the rhythm and tempo to create the effects you wish. Follow, as far as you are able, the rules of good grammar and correct spelling, but do not become preoccupied with details at this time. Let the *ideas* come out smoothly. They will tell the story.

It is far better to write too much than to write too little; it is easier to strike out superfluous words than to insert omitted ones. As you write this first draft, leave wide margins and space between lines so that you will have room for revisions. Put your citations of references in parentheses after the sentences to which they refer. When you rewrite, it will then be very simple to transform these brief notes into formal footnotes. Insert tables, figures, diagrams, charts, or maps wherever they will heighten interest or serve to clarify a point. If, however, you have a large mass of statistics or a long document which should be quoted in full, it is best to relegate this material to an appendix and refer the reader to it.

It is here, when writing your first draft, that you must be particularly careful to avoid *plagiarism*, which is defined as the act of taking and using as one's own the work of another writer (3). Plagiarism is sometimes unconscious and thus difficult to avoid, but every effort should be made to avoid it by giving credit where it is due.

Your bibliography may either be a part of your first draft, or it may be saved for later since you already have it in the form of your bibliography cards. Although your bibliography should be as comprehensive as possible, ordinarily it should include only books and articles you have actually consulted. Your references should be given in the conventional form as prescribed by your instructor.

Revising

When you have finished writing your first draft, it is advisable to set it aside for a few days, as you did with your outline. During these few days we recommend that you read some book on English style such as that by Strunk (4). Then reread your work critically. Does it possess direction and give a single controlling impression? If not, it may be possible to remedy the fault merely by eliminating an irrelevant paragraph or two. Sometimes it is necessary to write an additional paragraph to accomplish a smooth transition between major ideas. Often it is found that the order of the paragraphs should be changed. Sometimes this can be done best by using scissors and rubber cement rather than by re-copying entire paragraphs which may be satisfactory in themselves.

Read over your work critically, word by word, paying particular attention to your choice of words. As Mark Twain once said, "The difference between a word that is right and a word that is almost right is the difference between a firecracker and a soda cracker." You will find a good dictionary and a thesaurus almost indispensable in your search for exactly the right word. Pay attention also to the structure of your sentences. They must be grammatically effective, forceful and varied. You may be able to strengthen your writing by eliminating adjectives or even whole sentences that are not essential. Go over the entire paper several times, condensing and polishing it until it reads smoothly and persuasively. What is most important is that your ideas be transmitted to the reader. Careless writing blocks communication; careful writing fosters it.

Preparing the final copy

Your final copy should be neatly typed in the correct form. The original should be submitted in a cover or folder, and a carbon copy should be saved. The paper should bear your name, the course title and number, and the date that it is due. Do not neglect to proofread the final copy conscientiously before submitting it to your instructor. Even the best typists make mistakes, and carelessness in this final stage of your work can give a misleading impression of your entire effort. Follow through to the end; submit the paper before the deadline. Later, your carbon copy of the term paper should be punched in the same manner as your notebook paper and placed in a hard cover with your class notes.

Now, if you can afford the time, you are entitled to an extra evening off.

PREPARING ORAL ASSIGNMENTS

For it is not enough to know what we ought to say; we must also say it as we ought; much help is thus afforded towards producing the right impression of a speech.

Aristotle

The oral report, like all speech activities, is designed for communication. The speaker must first familiarize himself with the material for his assignment until he has the necessary information to present. Then he must relate his material to the interests of his audience. This means analyzing both his subject matter and his audience.

Once this problem is understood, the next step is to organize the material so as to make it both clear and interesting. A good outline is thus a necessity.

If the report is to be an extemporaneous one, that is, carefully prepared and rehearsed but neither written out nor memorized, the *key phrase* outline is the most serviceable. As you divide the subject matter into main and supporting issues, word these points in such a way that the phrases act as memory stimulants—phrases that do not tell you what you are to say, but remind you of what you planned to talk about.

Before your outline is completed, ask yourself how you can best get your audience's attention and arouse their interest for the information about to be given. Use an introduction that promises something worth hearing. The main part of your report follows. The conclusion is usually a summary. Since last impressions linger, you will want to make your summation clear and forceful.

The presentation should be rehearsed, using the outline, striving always to think ideas and not words. That is, the desire to get the ideas across clearly to the audience is a better motivation than concern with the words. This does not mean that you should not choose your words wisely; it only means that words are secondary in importance to ideas, and that you are constantly trying to find better ways of communicating the ideas.

If it is required that the report be written out, special attention should be paid to *style*. There is a difference between spoken and written rhythms, and since the report is to be interesting and clear in oral presentation, the style should resemble talking. Read the material aloud as you put it together. Listen to it critically. Does it sound as if you were really talking to your audience or does it have an artificial or "canned" sound?

When you present yourself to the audience, stand up tall and face them confidently; they are more apt to find it easy to listen. If you look as if you had something interesting to tell, an audience unconsciously reacts with a desire to listen and an expectation of something good to come. Let every member of the audience feel that he is being spoken to. Let your eyes have direct contact with the eyes of the audience. You will be stimulated by their reactions and they will feel that they are being spoken to—not talked at.

It is not necessary to speak very loudly for an audience to be able to follow you, but it is important that you project your voice to the back of the room. If you take time to shape your sounds a little more carefully than usual you will also be likely to speak a little more slowly, which is usually a good thing for your listeners. If your report is well put together it will not lack variety of ideas, but be sure that you have variety in the voice too—in tone quality, tempo and force.

Many types of reports can be improved by the use of visual aids. Pictures, graphs, maps, charts, or pertinent objects make the information more clear and interesting. No visual device should be used, however, unless it clearly adds to the effectiveness of the report. All visual aids should be large enough and graphic enough to be easily seen and understood by the audience, and should be displayed long enough for the audience to appreciate them.

Have something to say that is significant for your audience; arrange it in such a manner that it is easily followed; use your voice and any aids you have to make it interesting. **Communicate!**

PREPARING FOR A CLASS DISCUSSION

The two worst kinds of participants in a discussion are those who talk too much and those who do not talk enough. Between these two extremes are the good discussants, and they will usually be found to have the following characteristics:

First, they will be *well-informed*. One should prepare for a discussion as fully as one would for an individual speech. When you take part in a discussion, find out all you can about the subject ahead of time. Bring along notes with quotations, statistics, or any other pertinent data which you may want to introduce. Although you cannot prepare the exact words you are going to say, you can provide yourself with a solid background of material from which to draw.

A second characteristic of a good discussant is that he has an *open mind*. Although prepared, he is not dogmatic nor stubborn. If new evidence is introduced, he is ready to recognize it. If he honestly feels himself being persuaded with reason and logic, he will be sincere enough to admit it. The point in a discussion is not to win the argument but to find the best possible solution to a question.

This means *knowing how to think*. He must develop the capacity to weigh what he hears against what he knows already and to make decisions accordingly. On the one hand, he does not want to be wishy-washy and noncommittal, but on the other hand, he wants his observations to be based upon a healthy process of reflective thought, not merely on balkiness or on slowness in grasping the points of others.

A good discussion participant can be *objective* when objectivity is needed. Too many members of ineffectual discussions take remarks personally or assume that disagreement automatically means insult. They apply subjective values to what should be scientific or business-like. Learn to look squarely at the issue rather than at the personality attacking or defending the issue.

Naturally a good discussion member must be a particularly *good listener*. If speakers do not really hear one another, the interaction of group speech can only lead to greater isolation and antagonism. A person may assume ahead of time that someone else is going to take a particular position, and regardless of what that someone else actually does say, will act as though he had taken the preconceived position. Do not form too many notions about what others will say, or if you do, be prepared to **react to what you actually hear.**

A good member of a discussion also *sticks to the point*. He dare not be scatterbrained, for this affects the whole group. Too many people go off onto side issues. When you are attracted by one of these minor points during a discussion, develop the discipline to hold yourself back temporarily and try to get at the matter in hand. Otherwise, a discussion can easily degenerate into meaningless chatter and bickering.

One of the most important characteristics of a good discussant is that he is *courteous*. He does not constantly interrupt others, monopolize the floor, insult others with personal remarks, nor deliberately create heat and friction where there should be light and smoothness. He has good manners and a respect for others. This does not mean that he should refrain from disagreement or from stating his point of view with intensity. It means that he is as fair to others as he expects them to be to him.

NOTES TO CHAPTER 6

(1) Johann Frederich Herbart developed a five-step method of teaching early in the nineteenth century. Among the best known of recent five-step formulations for students is the "SQ3R" method, developed by F. P. Robinson in *Effective Study* (rev. ed.) (New York: Harper and Brothers, 1961), pp. 29-30. Another is the "PQRST" method of Thomas F. Staton, *How to Study* (Montgomery, Ala.: How to Study, 1954). Staton more recently developed an "R.S.V.P." formula. Still another variation is the "OK4R" method of Walter Pauk, *How to Study in College* (Boston: Houghton Mifflin Co., 1962).

(2) Luella Cole and Jessie Mary Ferguson, *Student's Guide to Effective Study* (New York: Holt, Rinehart & Winston, Inc., 1956), p. 47.

(3) Clarence L. Barnhart, *Thorndike-Barnhart Comprehensive Desk Dictionary* (New York: Doubleday and Co., Inc., 1958), p. 595.

(4) William Strunk, Jr., *Elements of Style,* rev. by E. B. White. (New York: Macmillan Paperbacks, MP107, 1962).

SUGGESTIONS FOR FURTHER READING AND REFERENCE

A Manual of Style (rev. ed.). Chicago: University of Chicago Press, 1949.

Campbell, William G., *Form and Style in Thesis Writing.* Boston: Houghton Mifflin Company, 1954.

Cooper, Charles W., and Edmund J. Robins, *The Term Paper, A Manual and Model.* (3rd ed.) Stanford, California: Stanford University Press, 1959.

Gilbert, Doris W., *Study in Depth.* New York: Prentice-Hall, Inc., 1966.

Linton, Calvin D., *How to Write Reports.* New York: Harper & Row, 1954.

New American Roget's College Thesaurus. New York: The New American Library, Signet D1431, 1961. See also: Pocket Book C13, and Washington Square Press W635.

Nicholson, Margaret (ed.), *Dictionary of American-English Usage Based on Fowler's Modern English Usage.* New York: The New American Library, Signet T1547. 1958.

Perrin, Porter G., *Writer's Guide and Index to English.* Chicago: Scott, Foresman and Co., 1952.

Roberts, Edgar V., *Writing Themes About Literature.* New York: Prentice-Hall, Inc., 1964.

Staton, Thomas F., *R.S.V.P. . . . a Dynamic Approach to Study.* Chicago: Scott, Foresman and Co., 1966.

Strunk, William, Jr., *Elements of Style,* rev. by E. B. White, New York: Macmillan Paperbacks, MP107, 1962.

Turabian, Kate L., *Manual for Writers of Term Papers, Theses, and Dissertations.* Chicago: Phoenix Books, p. 46, 1964.

VIEWPOINT

Learn How to Study
BY GOODWIN WATSON

Just how do our minds work when we study?
When you are reading is it ever a good idea to skip passages?
How can you keep your mind from wandering?
Is it always best to study alone?
Is it a sign of weakness to seek psychological help?

Poor students often have a false picture of learning as absorption. They look at a page in a book and expect somehow that page to impress itself on mind. It doesn't. Mind is not a container into which lectures or readings are poured. Mind is not a sponge, letting information seep into its pores. Mind is an organism at work. Knowledge comes out of experience. Passivity is an almost perfect defense against learning. Did you ever have the experience of listening to a long lecture, packed with knowledge, but containing one minor error which you happen to have spotted? If so, you may have been amused to notice that months later when you have forgotten even what the rest of the lecture was about, you remember the point which you challenged. Where you went into action, you learned.

Learn to Wrestle with a Book

The way to study a book is not to find a quiet spot and an easy chair, to light your pipe, and then placidly turn the pages of the book, waiting for its ideas to come out and affect you. Good learning involves more of a wrestle with a book. The best study is a constant challenge and reaction to what the author is saying. Sometimes it's a help to visualize the writer speaking out of the printed page. Always it is useful to come at a book with questions in mind. Reading is a check-up rather than a lap-up job. You may begin with the Table of Contents. Poor students usually skip this. The good student wants an over-all view; first he wants to plan where he's going. He gets from the "Table of Contents" an idea of the several main sections. He sees then the pattern by which the author has outlined the whole job. The student asks himself then where the heart of the book's contribution to him is likely to lie. Perhaps there will be long sections of introduction which are not necessary in order to get the author's essential idea. Or, the book may be written with the central thesis presented in the early chapters, so they must be read with care, while later chapters apply the

Dr. Watson at the time of this article was a professor at Teachers College, Columbia University. This viewpoint was published in the *Intercollegian*. Reprinted by permission.

viewpoint in various fields, some of which are important to the reader and others of which can be glanced over lightly.

Judicious Art of Skipping

The mature college student will find in most books in most fields a large amount of repetition of things he already knows. He can save time by judicious skipping. The Table of Contents and the sub-heads within each chapter give a fairly good idea of what the author plans to say. A quick check-up will show whether or not he is developing the discussion about as you imagined he would. This is *active* study. You are ahead of the book. You are thinking about the problem, are aware of what you already know, and are concentrating on getting the fresh, new contribution from the writer. You will probably find that using this active, questioning, challenging, selective approach, you can read three books in the time it used to take you to read one by the traditional method of beginning at the top of the first page and reading every word from beginning to end. You will not only cover more ground but you will have learned more from each book read. Because your mind has been at work on the material, you are more likely to remember it. You remember what you have DONE.

End Determines Means

Keep tests in mind. Athletic coaches may use a slow-motion picture to let the learner see for himself what he is doing and where he departs from the desired form. In many college courses, evaluation waits for a mid-term or final examination. Then it is too late. The good student must find some devices by which he can test his progress as he goes along. Too often a man says to himself, "Oh, I know that perfectly, but I just didn't think of it at the time." The knowledge was available if asked for in one way, but didn't connect with the situation in which it was needed.

So then, tests a student applies to his learning should be related to his purpose in studying that particular material. If you are learning something just to pass a multiple-choice, objective type examination, then the best way to test progress is to form a partnership with some other students, to make up questions of the type you are likely to have to answer, try them out on one another, and to correct the errors. If you are preparing primarily to pass an examination which will require that you reproduce in an essay the principal ideas presented in lectures and textbook, then one of the best tests is to try to outline each major topic of the course, with all the proper headings and sub-heads under each. If you can reproduce a full and correct outline from memory, you will be able to use it in writing your examination. If you are to be tested for skill in solving certain problems, you can make up problems for yourself and use them in practice tests. It seems to be especially true in learning mathematics or statistics that a point will seem clear as day in class, but confusion enters when the student tries later to use what he has learned in solving a typical example.

Of course, it would be a mistake to limit the testing process to classroom quizzes. The college degree is doubtless useful, but the main concern ought to be with what education does to improve the quality of living. That is the important test to be applied at any stage of education.

Tricks to Treasure

A word now about over-learning. The need for over-learning arises because we forget so much so quickly. If you are learning a list of irregular verbs in French, and have each on a separate card, you will practice them until you can say them once correctly. But that is not enough. Drill beyond the point of being able to struggle through the list. Get it down cold; don't leave it on the false assumption that when it has once been learned you are through.

Mnemonic devices are sometimes helpful; but largely on the same principle that any creative use of what is being learned deepens its impression. You may remember the correct order of the several French and Indian wars by using the first letter of each to form a word. You may be able to construct a single vivid mental picture which incorporates a series of persons or events so that one feature of their relationship is easily recalled. Sometimes a troublesome distinction can be given a twist of meaning that makes it stick. For example, one man, probably a woman-hater, remembers that Frances is a girl and Francis is a boy because the "e" has an empty head. The rhyme, "Thirty days hath September," is a well-known mnemonic device for keeping lengths of months in mind. Other people use the knuckles of two fists to count off the long and short months. Psychologists recognize that devices of this kind are occasionally helpful, but believe it would be wasteful to construct elaborate memory systems for all one wishes to recall. The inventing and application of the memory aids may take more time than would be required for direct learning by practicing recall.

Think, Live at Your Best

A common problem in studying is mind-wandering. Sometimes this arises from lack of adequate motivation. Your mind doesn't wander if you are hungry and on your way to a meal. Sometimes a too-long period of study at one task becomes wasteful. Shorter periods with more intense concentration are more profitable than long hours with a book in which one finds himself eventually reading words that have no meaning. The most important fact to remember about mind-wandering, however, is that your thoughts usually wander *to* rather than wander *from*. They are apt to be directed more or less unconsciously toward some goal. A good cure for mind-wandering is this: Put a pad of paper beside your work. Whenever you discover that your mind isn't on your work, note down on that pad just what was passing through your thoughts at the moment. Be honest with yourself. Turn back to your work. Next time your thoughts stray, again note their direction. Write it down. Keep this up. When a sizable list begins to accumulate, the problem of readjustment will begin to clear. If you find you keep thinking of a number of things you mustn't forget to do, you may be able to clear the deck for action by putting aside your study for a moment and making yourself a schedule with definite times for getting done all those troublesome obligations. The plan to do them may release the tension which constantly pulls them into mind.

Students sometimes ask whether it is better to study alone or to study in pairs and in groups. The answer is that a judicious combination of individual work and group work is better than either alone. Discussion of problems and answers in a group usually brings out more aspects than any individual of the group would have thought of by himself. Arguments arising in the group bring a chance to apply what has been read, and by their intensity deepen the memory impression. The group also, as suggested above, provides a good chance to test one another. On the other hand, it would usually be wasteful to read expository material aloud in a group. Tasks of translation, math problems, or creative writing are better done by each for himself and then reviewed and criticized in a small friendly group. The individual must be careful never to come to rely on other members of his group for results that he is some day going to have to be able to get for himself.

Then, some students with good ability fail in school because of emotional conflicts. Perhaps something inside them won't let them succeed. One brilliant young fellow used to write superb papers which he would tear up on a sudden impulse just before he was supposed to hand them in. He felt unworthy of the success he knew they would bring him. Another fellow was studying medicine—and doing very poorly. As he talked to a psychological counselor he discovered, to his own surprise, how much the choice of medicine had been his father's rather than his own. He was unconsciously expressing resentment against his father's domination by getting grades which distressed his father. In his chosen field of architecture the same boy had no trouble doing excellent work.

Many colleges today have people prepared to help with the problems of personality readjustment—psychiatrists, or deans, or personnel officers, or psychological counselors. We all get involved in difficult situations in our own emotional lives, and this is true also of the persons who seem well-adjusted and successful. At such times, a little friendly counsel from someone who views us more objectively than we can view ourselves is very helpful. It is no more a disgrace or a sign of weakness to seek psychological help than it is to go to a dentist for an aching tooth.

Above all, a balanced life, with time for play and time for sleep and normally attractive meals, should serve as a foundation for efficient study. When you don't live right, it's hard to think straight. Scholarship purchased at the cost of health is a poor bargain. In this, as in many other matters, it is well to regard school as life, rather than as preparation for life. The years spent in college are an important part of your three-score-years-and-ten. To distort life today is poor preparation for any good tomorrows. It is just as important to live at your best during college years as it will be during any other years of your one short life.

CHAPTER 7

Can You Get More Out of the Lectures?

"The power of attention is the mark of a civilized man," said Lord Chesterfield, and going to college requires you to spend considerable time in paying attention and just listening. Most people, however, find it difficult to listen to anything for very long. And unless a person has trained himself carefully he will tend to select from what he hears only the material that fits his own previous experiences. Fortunately, there is some evidence that skill in listening can be improved by training. In this chapter we will discuss how you can make yourself a better listener and thereby increase your efficiency as a student.

LISTEN TO THE LECTURE

There are three main elements in the classroom situation: you, the instructor, and the subject matter. We will begin with the element over which you have the most control—you.

You

In order to listen intelligently you must become "involved," physically, emotionally, and mentally. You can involve yourself *physically* by taking notes, sitting up, and focusing your attention on the instructor. In contrast, poorer students often slump in their chairs and let their attention wander.

You can become involved *emotionally* by an earnest desire to learn something, whether it is because you are intensely interested in the subject or for other reasons. The better student expects to find the lecture interesting, and he is seldom disappointed. The poorer student usually comes to class prepared to be bored. It is a rare lecturer who can inspire him under such circumstances, and so the poor student's expectations usually come true.

> *A good listener is not only popular everywhere, but after a while he knows something.*
>
> Wilson Mizner

You can become involved *mentally* by conscientiously reading your assignments in advance, making a critical evaluation of what your instructor is saying, and trying to relate his words to what you already know. It is a mistake merely to "soak up" indiscriminately everything he says. Thinking ahead of the speaker and trying to guess what will come next also will help to keep you mentally involved in the lecture. Remember that thought is much faster than speech so a listener often "tunes himself out." If you do this, be sure to tune in again quickly.

Even if you have not prepared yourself in advance by studying the day's assignment, you still can derive considerable benefit by paying careful attention in class. Obviously, it is much more efficient to study your lessons in advance. An early arrival in class gives you an opportunity to review your notes from the previous lecture and to become mentally prepared for what is to come.

The instructor

Students sometimes feel hostile toward their instructors. Such feelings may exist at an unconscious level but nevertheless interfere with learning. Why should a student who comes to learn, dislike the instructor who is there solely to help him learn? There are several possibilities. Perhaps the student has already developed an attitude of resistance and distrust toward *anyone* who seems to be in authority. As a result he tries to do as little as possible and that little only when he is forced to. Such a student feels abused and under pressure. He complains about assignments, resists suggestions, even those that might be helpful, and feels relief when he can get away. An insecure student may hold back, instead of participating in class, fearing that he will be exposed at any minute to public scorn.

Instructors are human beings. Students generally find this basic fact as difficult to accept as the similar truth that their own parents are also human beings, with strengths and weaknesses, virtues and faults, certainties and confusions, just like other people.

It is the task of the student to extract from this mortal instructor the ageless wisdom it is hoped he possesses. Ignore—as far as you can—any personal peculiarities of your instructor and try instead to concentrate on his *ideas*. It is also essential that you learn something about his general *method of lecturing*.

Many instructors begin each lecture with a summary of the previous ones. They may also try at this time to clarify subjects which they believe were not treated adequately in the preceding lecture. For this reason the first few minutes of a talk are often very important. Here, the instructor tries to select the material he considers essential for you to learn. Similarly, the conclusion of the lecture is important. Lecturers sometimes discover that the minutes have passed too quickly, that they have spent too much time in illustrations and examples, and so they speed up at the end. Thus a large part of the planned lecture may have to be condensed into those last few minutes when some of the less interested students have already started gathering up their books, looking for their shoes, and preparing to leave.

Students often complain that an instructor is not interesting or exciting. Although, alas, this may indeed be true of some instructors, there are several points you should bear in mind. Just as beauty is in the eye of the beholder, interest is in the mind of the student. Obviously, there can be no uninteresting speaker without an uninterested listener. If you are this listener, it is your obligation to make the necessary changes for yourself—in yourself. The most qualified teachers are not necessarily the most exciting ones. What counts is how much learning takes place in their students. In fact, the most brilliant and interesting lecturer is not always as *effective* as one would expect. His presentation may be so persuasive and stimulating that the student is swept along unquestioningly, yet is later unable to understand just how he was convinced.

When your instructors invite questions they are usually sincere. Often, the same question that is troubling you may be bothering other students. The one person who asks the unsettled question thus makes a contribution on behalf of the entire class. It is worthwhile to write down questions as they occur to you. Later, you can write in the answers as they appear in the lecture or in your reading. If your questions should not be answered in due course, be sure to follow them up by further reading, by discussions with other students, or by asking your instructor who will usually be glad to see you, especially during his scheduled office hours. The question you simply let go may not die. It may rise from the grave of time past and reappear like a zombie to stalk you on examination day.

The subject

According to some students, each subject they studied seemed to have a peculiar structure and language of its own. Despite their best efforts, certain subjects seemed to elude them, but they usually found that if they were persistent and studied hard enough, they were able to do well enough to get by. Sometimes, after intensive effort, they were able to make a significant "breakthrough" in understanding. After this, everything fell into place and became meaningful to them. Before the breakthrough they could only pile fact upon fact, generalization upon generalization. Once they gained a real grasp of the subject, they found it easy to incorporate new material into what they already knew.

You can improve your grasp of subject matter by relating the topic you are studying to the over-all plan of the course, and by trying to find reasons for the sequence of topics. The course itself should be placed in relation to other courses in the same field. Think also of your own reasons for wanting to understand the subject.

TAKE NOTES FOR YOUR OWN USE

There are rare students who have such powers of concentration and memory that they never have to take notes in class. The general experience, however, is that students who get good grades have taken good notes.

In order to determine whether note-taking is necessary, an experiment was conducted which involved college students who attended one particular series of lectures. One group of students was not permitted to take notes, while the other was required to write down the main points of each lecture. In a test given immediately after the close of the series, the group that had been required to take notes made higher scores than the group that did not take notes. The same test was repeated without warning two weeks later. The difference was even greater this time, and still in favor of the group which had been required to take notes. This investigation indicated that for most people note-taking is a valuable tool for mastering the material in a course. Yet, in a study made at another institution, most of the freshman class did not know how to take notes when they entered college. This section will explain exactly what good notes can do for you and then give you some practical suggestions which many other students have found helpful.

Your purpose

The first purpose of taking notes is to make the main points of the lecture available to you again in a *convenient form*. Most students are not able to retain more than a small amount of what a good lecturer can say in fifty minutes. With your notes, you can go over the material as often as you wish. Second, your notes will help you *organize your learning* by placing the points in a logical sequence and by highlighting the main ones. Third, you may learn from your lecturer *material which is not readily available* from other sources. Thus, the notes you compile will be very helpful as a basis for your original study of the subject. Then as examination time approaches, at a terrifying velocity, your notes will become priceless for *purposes of review*. It may be that many instructors try to give their students valuable *specific clues* as to what will actually be asked in the examination, but somehow it seems that only a few members of the class notice this or get much benefit from it.

Taking notes forces you to pay attention in class. When taking useful notes you must constantly analyze the lecturer's thoughts. In this way, you become an active participant in what is going on in class.

Practical advice

The only good notes are those which can be read and understood by the person who made them *whenever he needs them*. No matter what method is used or what ingenious measures are taken to save effort, notes must *be meaningful later to their writer*. Above all, notes should be written legibly and with plenty of white space between the lines. When considering any advice on note-taking, remember that *what you are trying to do is to develop the best system for yourself by selecting or discarding the advice of others*. Once you begin to use your own system you will want to keep improving it as you become more experienced. How well you take and use notes may make the difference between your success or your failure in college.

BEGIN WITH THE RIGHT EQUIPMENT

Your notebook

Use a standard 8-1/2 x 11, 3-ring looseleaf notebook of good quality. This is convenient, readily available, and used in most colleges. Any duplicated material the instructor may distribute to the class will probably be designed for an 8-1/2 x 11 notebook. Write your name, address, and phone number inside the cover.° Use only one side of the paper. (Index cards and odd scraps of paper are sometimes used for lecture notes. They get lost. Odd-sized notebooks may be distinctive, but the supplies of fillers or organizers have a way of disappearing from the bookstore just when you need them.) We recommend that you use just *one* notebook with the different courses separated by dividers. (This way, you cannot snatch the wrong notebook as you rush to class.) Finally, keep your notebook neat and free from anything which does not belong in it.

Your calendar page

One other suggestion that can save you a world of grief is to **write all of your assignments for all courses in one place** instead of keeping them only with the notes for the particular course. For this purpose you may use a calendar page in the front of your notebook, or a date book which you can carry with you. This practice is valuable not only for daily reading assignments but also for such long-term obligations as term papers. Anything you cannot finish in one session ought to have several dates set for checking on your progress. For example, if a term paper is due in a few months, decide how long you can spend on choosing a topic, how long on reading, outlining, writing, revising, and typing. Then translate these periods of time into dates on your calendar. In this way, you can always tell whether you are going to the dance with a clear or a bad conscience.

Your pen

Use a ball-point or fountain pen with blue-black or black ink. This is

---

° Girls attending co-educational colleges sometimes write this information on the outside of the cover. The effects of this have not yet been studied by educational psychologists.

legible and permanent. (Pencils smudge. Colored inks are distracting and difficult to read.)

SELECT THE MAIN IDEAS

The two keys to successful notetaking are to **select** and to **organize.** Your first objective is to select the most important ideas presented in the lecture as well as the most important details relating to these ideas. But how can you tell which are the main ideas? One way is by preparing yourself for the lecture by reading ahead. Once this is done, the day's lecture will not burst upon you as a complete surprise and you will be ready to recognize important points as they turn up. Watch particularly for points on which your instructor may differ with the authors of the readings.

Your instructor wants you to get the best possible notes from his lecture and he may try in several ways to point out the main ideas to you. Often, he will have a number of these major concepts for each lecture—perhaps three, but sometimes as many as twelve or more. He will try to emphasize these points by his tone of voice and perhaps by gestures or pauses. He will usually repeat these major ideas several times; when you hear something repeated which is not in your notes, put it in! Your instructor may also restate the same idea in several different ways. One excellent guidebook for college instructors (1) cites Spencer in this connection, "It is only by varied reiteration that unfamiliar truths are forced upon reluctant minds." Any concept which is repeated several times definitely deserves a place in your notes and, more importantly, in your mind.

Your instructor will also indicate important points by stressing "topic sentences" in his introduction and in his summary. He will often use "cue" expressions such as:

> **It is important to know that . . .**
> **The best explanation is . . .**
> **The term is defined as . . .**
> **Most authorities agree that . . .**
> **There are three factors in . . .**

(In your notes write: **"3 factors in . . . "** and then **number** each one, so that you do not miss any.)

Other important "cue" expressions often overlooked by students are: *therefore, moreover, however, likewise, first, to begin with, finally, nevertheless, furthermore.*

Sometimes, the instructor will say explicitly:

> **"Remember this, . . ."** or even,
> **"Get this! You'll see it again on the final."**

In spite of all the signs, repetitions, and admonitions, there are always students who miss these very points in the final examination.

Another way for an instructor to emphasize important points is by use of the chalkboard. **Almost anything your instructor writes on the board is worth copying.** Obviously, this includes lists, assignments, and diagrams, but even if he merely draws a slanting line and says, "The general trend is upward," copying the line into your notebook may help you to remember the idea.

Be sure to take careful notes of any statements that strike you as ridiculous, or that conflict with your present beliefs and desires. Many studies show that such ideas are the most apt to be ignored, forgotten or misconstrued by the listener (2).

Be precise

It is essential that your lecture notes at all times accurately reflect the ideas of the speaker. Be specially watchful for such *qualifying expressions* as:

> **There is some evidence that . . .**
> **From the few samples studied . . .**
> **Some authorities believe . . .**
> **My hunch is . . .**
> **There seems to be a tendency for . . .**

Questions on examinations often require you to distinguish among general principles, verifiable facts, and mere opinions. Be sure your notes reflect the distinctions.

Write statements

In writing down the important points, it is essential that you express them as brief statements and not as mere topic headings. Your notes should be complete and meaningful in themselves, although they need not be in the form of grammatical sentences. Which of these two examples of notes do you think would be more useful to you as you study for an examination a month after the lecture?

> (a)   **James Joyce, born Dublin, 1882**
> (b)   **Birthdate of James Joyce**

Write the correct amount

Try to write a quantity of notes which is *appropriate* to the subject and to your own knowledge. The amount for a fifty-minute lecture may vary from a half-page for a subject which emphasizes broad concepts to three or four pages for a subject in which details are very important.

Remember that your notes should serve you. Do not let yourself become a slave to them by writing so much that you cannot learn while you are writing. After all, a lecture is intended to be a learning situation and the wise student uses it as such. For this reason, the taking of full notes in shorthand is not recommended. Good stenographers write automatically, taking everything down without conscious thought. This is the exact opposite of the selective process we recommend for taking lecture notes. For the same reason, tape-recording lectures is of little value.

You are the only one who can tell whether you are writing the correct amount of notes for yourself, but here are some criteria which can help you decide. If at the end of the hour you are exhausted because you have been writing frantically all the time, and if you still find that you cannot understand what you have written, it is clear that you have written too much. If you have not found it necessary to take many notes in class, yet all sorts of items about which you are rather hazy keep appearing in the quizzes, it is apparent that you are not taking enough notes for that particular subject, or at least not enough for *your* knowledge of the subject.

It is best to listen first and then write. If you miss a point, just leave some space and keep going. You will be able to pick it up later. Be sure to mark with an asterisk or a question mark in the margin any point you do not fully understand, including facts or spellings you will want to check later.

Some writers suggest that you take notes fairly constantly all during the lecture; others urge that you write only when some significant point has been made. This is a matter for you to decide for yourself.

Whose words?

Opinion is also divided on the question of whether you ought to take notes in your own words or in the lecturer's words. The main advantage of using your own words, according to some instructors, is that it is somewhat more likely that you will understand what you are writing. One disadvantage of using your own words is that it is more time-consuming, and you also run the serious danger of misinterpreting the speaker. This is particularly true when he is discussing a subject about which you already have strong preconceptions or prejudices, or for which your knowledge is neither full nor exact. For this reason, some instructors prefer that whatever notes you take be as literal as possible.

ORGANIZE THE MAIN IDEAS

Order is Heav'n's first Law

Alexander Pope

It is not easy to take down someone else's thoughts in a logical order during a lecture. But the ability to take good notes and arrange them systematically comes as the result of experience and effort. You can see the relationship of various ideas to each other more easily by using an outline form for your notes. This is very important, for the *ability to grasp relationships* is fundamental in learning.

Use the outline style

Although there are at least seven different styles used for taking notes, we recommend only one to you, the *idea-outline*. You begin by writing the title of the lecture. Then write a brief statement of the first major idea beginning at the left margin of the page. Indent every statement which supports, explains, or is subordinate to this major idea. Put statements of equal or coordinate value on the same line of indentation. If you wish, you may use conventional symbols for each level of subordination. It is unusual to need more than three levels for lecture notes, but we shall include here all six which are commonly used in more elaborate outlines:

I.
II.
  A.
  B.
    1.
    2.
      a.
      b.
        1)
        2)
          a)
          b)

See Figures 1 and 2 for examples of the use of the idea-outline for lecture notes in biology and literature.

Do not neglect to include enough specific facts or details so that you can illustrate and apply the main ideas. Details will help you to remem-

III. Phylum Coelenterata ("hollow gut")
  A. all aquatic, mostly marine, attached or floating
  B. Two forms of individual
    1. Polyp, sessile, cylindrical, often in colonies
    2. Medusa, free-floating, bell-like, not in colonies
  C. 3 classes
    1. Hydrozoa - 3700 species; some fresh water,
       polyps and medusae, e.g. Hydra.

    2. Scyphozoa (= jellyfish) - 200 sp., all marine,
       mostly medusae, e.g. Aurelia *

    3. Anthozoa (= corals, sea anemones) -
       6100 sp., all marine, all polyps,
       e.g. Coralium, Metridium.

                                    * Check spelling

Figure 1
Example of Notes for Biology

I. THE 2 TYPES OF POETRY
  A. Narrative
    1. Aim is to tell a story
    2. Structure
      a. Development (certainty of conflict
         becomes definite)
      b. Turning point (= climax)
      c. Denouement (unraveling of action,
         problem is answered)
    3. Kinds
      a. Epic - long, serious, grand-scale
         story
      b. Ballad - song-like story
      c. Dramatic monologue - story told in
         own words of speaker
      d. Romance - tender, antique story
  B. lyric

                    * learn one example of each!

Figure 2
Example of Notes for Literature

ber the major concepts and you can sometimes actually reconstruct a principle by thinking of a few examples.

Two common faults to be avoided in making outlines are dividing the topic too finely, so that the outline gets "strung out," and the opposite, "cluttering" the items so that they become difficult to read or understand.

When it is not possible to make a logical outline of the lecture material, a **"psychological" outline** can be followed. This implies a process whereby one important idea naturally leads to another important idea and so on. In this way a chain of ideas which will hang together whenever material is needed again is formed in the mind of the student. The main difficulty seen in many students' notes is that there is *neither* logical nor psychological coherence. The important point is that you organize your notes so that they make sense to you.

Asides and irrelevancies

Sometimes your instructor will go into a long discussion of a topic which does not appear at the time to be relevant to the subject at hand. Your notes on this discussion should be enclosed in a box or circle. If you find out where they belong later, you may be able to draw an arrow to the correct place. If, on the other hand, it turns out that the discussion really is irrelevant, you can ignore it as you follow your outline. Your lecturer's "asides," jokes, and odd *obiter dicta* can be handled similarly if for some reason you wish to remember them.

FOLLOW A FORM

Several forms for taking notes have been suggested by various writers. Some recommend that you rule your page vertically into two or three columns. In the two-column system, you use the left half of the page for rough notes taken in class, and the right half for a refined outline written later or for only the most important general principles. The three-column or "2-5-1" system described by Walter Pauk, (3) saves a two-inch column at the left of the page for a later brief summary of the lecture. The lecture itself is recorded in the five-inch center column, and a one-inch column at the right is available for your own ideas. Pauk also suggests a "2-3-3-2" form for lectures which are closely based on an assigned text. In this form, one first writes his textbook notes in the middle three-inch column, then writes his lecture notes in the right-hand three-inch column, and uses the two-inch space at the left for a summary. A two-inch space at the bottom is reserved for later reflection and synthesis.

Ehrlich (4) recommends that you write on only one side of the page, and use the blank side of the preceding page for special entries concerning your study needs. For example, you might write a note to yourself to reread a particular chapter or to look up the definition of a term.

Once you have chosen a form that suits your needs, it is best to stay with it, at least for a particular course. Although you should try to improve your skill at taking notes, do not risk success in a course by experimenting with widely divergent methods.

Headings

Begin each day's notes with the course number and the date. If there is more than one instructor, write the name of the lecturer each day. Otherwise, writing the name once on the first day will be sufficient. Skip several lines between each day's notes. Letter your main topic headings or "headlines" in capitals centered on a line of the page. Subordinate headings should be printed at the left side of the page, following the style of this book.

Abbreviations

Most people find that the use of abbreviations and symbols is necessary if they are going to keep up with the speaker. The indiscriminate use of abbreviations, however, can lead to the most frustrating kind of puzzle for you just when you are not in the mood for puzzles. One effective way of abbreviating words is to omit the vowels. Thus, "trnsfr" can readily be seen to mean "transfer" and "yrs" can mean "yours," or "years." The suffix "ing" can be represented by plain "g" as in "trnsfrg." Generally, you can use any other symbols or abbreviations you know, such as those listed below:

fr = from	cf. = compare, see
w = with	re = in reference to
w/o = without	vs. = against
e.g. = for example	N.B. = note well!
!! = important	? = query or
sic = thus it was in	questionable item
the original	∴ = therefore
i.e. = that is	∵ = since
➡ = produces, or	etc. = and so forth
results in	Q. = question
⬅ = derived from	ref. = reference

You can also save time by using initials for names which are used frequently. If an entire lecture is about William Shakespeare, for example, it is sufficient to spell out the name once at the top of the page and abbreviate subsequent repetitions of the name *on that page* as "Sh," or "WS." Otherwise, it is advisable to keep a list of your own original abbreviations along with their interpretations on a special page in the front of your notebook.

USE YOUR NOTES EFFECTIVELY

After class

The best time for you to fill in any extra material which you remember but did not have time to write is *immediately after the lecture.* This is also an excellent time for you to edit or rewrite portions of your notes, if necessary. Pay special attention to any doubtful items you indicated by question marks in the margin.

Opinion is divided as to whether it is worthwhile to rewrite or copy your notes completely. Apparently this is an individual matter, although it may depend somewhat more upon the lecturer than upon the student. That is, if a lecturer does not work from a clear outline, the student is more likely to find it necessary to edit and rewrite his notes. We believe, however, that whenever possible, it should be your goal to take notes in a final form right in the classroom.

A good way to improve your notes after class is to get together with a few serious classmates and go over them together. One student reads his notes aloud while the others follow his reading in their own notes, being alert for errors and omissions. Any questionable points are discussed immediately and settled if possible. At the next session someone else reads. At some universities, the practice is to make later additions and corrections to your notes in pencil or in another color of ink so that long afterwards you can tell what *you* actually heard in class. By the way, a coffee-shop, a lawn, or someone's room are all better for this purpose than the reading room of your college library.

Assuming that you have done all this and have produced notes which are clear, legible, and appropriate, how do you actually make use of them?

According to Arthur Volle, (5) one of the characteristics that distinguishes good students from poor ones is that many more of the good students make a practice of reviewing their lecture notes *within the first few hours following the lecture.* Because we forget rapidly at first, reading the notes promptly reinforces the learnings of the lecture period.

This saves the time which would be necessary for relearning from the beginning.

Before class

It is a well-established principle of psychology that we learn more in several short periods of time than in a single lengthy period. This, of course, applies to the studying of lecture notes. One brief period which is particularly valuable for studying is the five or ten minutes immediately before class begins. This practice not only orients you to the day's work but also helps you get into a receptive frame of mind so that you can learn more. In addition to the few minutes before class, you will want to devote a portion of your time schedule every day to studying your lecture notes for each course. You will also use your lecture notes in your weekly, monthly, and final intensive reviews before examination.

Lending your notes

If someone missed a lecture and wants to use your notes, see that they are kept in your presence while they are being used. You can replace a textbook which is borrowed and not returned but your own notes are like your own teeth. Substitutes are available but they are rarely as good as the originals.

After the course is over

After you have finally completed a course, by all means place your notes in a hard-cover binder, label them, and keep them permanently. You may want to refer to them again in another course and, besides, there they stand: permanent evidence of how hard you studied when you went to college.

PARTICIPATE

Attend class

There are many plausible reasons for not attending class, and a student who really tries can produce any number of excellent excuses for cutting:

"I don't feel so well today."
"I can spend my time more productively elsewhere."
"That instructor bores me."

"I've got to prepare for another class."
"This is the only possible time I could make the appointment."
"Everyone cuts once in a while and I've been good so far this term."
"Who can possibly stay in class on a day like this?"

Nevertheless, the cold, hard fact remains that cutting class is one of the outstanding characteristics of students who fail. In one study (6) it was found that more than half the failing students had six or more cuts.

In contrast to the many reasons for not attending class, there are only a few reasons for attending. But these few reasons are extremely compelling. At the lowest level, we have seen that while faithful attendance in class does not guarantee a passing grade, it does make one more likely for most students. At a somewhat higher level, class attendance is almost always the most economical way to invest the time you have available for learning. It is only good sense, therefore, to attend class and to get as much as you can from it.

Be active

You will get much more from class if you are attentive and active. Listen not only to remember but also in order to go beyond what you are hearing. Try, for example, to relate what you learn in one class with what you have learned in other classes or in other previous experiences. Be on the alert for sudden insights or new understandings.

It is helpful to imagine the opposite of the argument presented by the lecturer; provided, of course, that you first understand what he is trying to say. The trouble with many students is that they never critically examine the lecturer's ideas. Nor do they examine their own ideas even when they are being directly challenged.

Since education is change, you ought to ask yourself in what way, if any, you are being changed by each particular session of a class.

Volunteer to recite

Instructors are generally more alert to what is going on in class than students believe. Among other things, instructors watch for evidence that the student is interested and trying to learn. One of the ways students indicate this is by asking relevant questions and by volunteering to recite. Studies show that the students who get superior grades more often are those who frequently offer to recite in class. There is an additional advantage to speaking up in class. Trying to think of something interesting and appropriate to say is an excellent way of keeping up your own interest and alertness. In short, it is one of the best ways for you to **participate.**

On the other hand, avoid talking too much in class. Unless the instructor definitely encourages you to continue, you should probably confine your voluntary contributions to not more than one or two for each class session. These contributions should be brief and to the point. If it seems that you are starting to compete for time with the instructor, or if your classmates sigh and groan when you start to speak, you may well suspect it is time to cut down.

NOTES TO CHAPTER 7

(1) Robly D. Evans, (Chairman), *You and Your Students* (Cambridge, Massachusetts: Massachusetts Institute of Technology, 1950).
(2) Virginia Voeks, *On Becoming an Educated Person* (Philadelphia, Pennsylvania: W. B. Saunders Co., 1964), pp. 64-65.
(3) Walter Pauk, *How to Study in College* (Boston: Houghton Mifflin Co., 1962), pp. 24-30.
(4) Eugene H. Ehrlich, *How to Study Better and Get Higher Marks* (New York: Thomas Y. Crowell Co., 1961), pp. 66-67.
(5) Arthur H. Volle, *Comparison of Academically Most Successful and Least Successful College Freshmen* (Evanston, Ill.: Ph.D. dissertation, Northwestern University, August, 1952).
(6) *Ibid.*

VIEWPOINT

How to Educate Yourself Even Though You Are Going to College

BY LYNN WHITE, JR.

What should be the job of the college student?
Does it pay to shop around for courses?
Can a person graduate without learning how to read properly?
Why is writing ability so important?
Do men listen differently from women?

One of the best-educated women I have ever known never went to college. Indeed, she didn't get much beyond grade school. The result of this seeming misfortune was anything but a misfortune: she knew that she had to educate herself. She became a voracious reader of books—not just magazines—and when she got steamed up about an idea or a subject she read and read until she really knew something "in depth" about it. She deliberately trained herself to be a brilliant conversationalist in the sense that she knew how to collect interesting people around her and then, without herself saying too much, how to get them talking and how to keep the ideas and insights flowing. And when there was a pause or a convergence of ideas, she could lead the talk to another level. She was able to do all this because when she got interested in anthropology she read Kroeber; when a friend got involved in Plotinus she read Dean Inge to find out what the shouting was all about; when she got entranced with psychic research she plunged into Sir Oliver Lodge and Stewart Edward White.

Why is it that relatively so few graduates of our colleges and universities live the life of the mind in this way? I think one important reason is that the American propensity for buying packaged products and Nationally Advertised Brands often deceives students, not to mention their parents, into thinking that if they "go to college" they have bought a certified commodity. But buying an education is more like buying a painting than like buying an automobile. Your automobile will get you places, but the best of paintings won't do anything for you except variegate your wall space unless you work hard and continuously to probe the artist's intention. You can part with a lot of money in the process of getting an education but you can't buy an education. All you can do is buy yourself an exposure to an education.

Dr. White, formerly president of Mills College (California) is professor of history at the University of California at Los Angeles. During 1965 he was associated with the Institute for Advanced Study at Princeton University. This article addressed to young women is reprinted from *Mademoiselle*, © Street and Smith Publications, Inc., August 1958, 241 ff.

Another reason it is hard to get a real education in college is the need of some students to demonstrate their superiority by pretending that they are bored to extinction. Unfortunately, a good many bright-eyed freshmen, eager to grow up and naturally looking for models, decide that they too should be bored, since obviously boredom is a sign of maturity.

Moreover, the merchandising instincts of America and the heavy competition among colleges and universities to attract topflight students have propagated the Gimmick Theory of education. The catalogues of our institutions are spangled and bangled with fascinating curriculums, plans for independent reading, honors courses, junior years in Europe or Mexico or Utopia, junior semesters in Washington, provisions for "leisured learning," devices for inciting the "gifted" student. Even the more creaky of such academic mechanisms have the merit of keeping our thinking flexible, and a few may turn out to be important. (For example, at U.C.L.A. last autumn tests turned up ninety-four "frosh" who placed nationally in the upper one-half of 1 per cent in intelligence, and two could have skipped straight from high school into graduate work. Naturally, all of these were put into studies that would give them a run for their money.) But you are going to get an education, as distinct from a diploma, only in terms of your own plan, which you work out for yourself, which from time to time you alter for yourself in the light of your widening interests and experience, and to which you have a personal commitment that is almost religious in its intensity and in its dedication to something more than yourself.

This does not mean that, come the autumn, you will march up to the Registrar's Office of your chosen Grove of Academe and announce: "I am enrolling for this and this and this." "Self-expression" is a catchword of our time, and those of us who use it most glibly sometimes forget that a self that is as yet only very partially discovered is usually a self scarcely worth expressing. The world of teachers and scholars has learned that students coming to college seldom have much notion either of the extent of the skills that an educated person must master or the range of human interests with which a person must have at least fleeting contact before he can really say: "Of all the colors in the spectrum, this is the one that puts a glint in *my* eye!"

Let me suggest a few habits in terms of which you can work out your own very personal plan for educating yourself. They are habits of mind and of action that will fit the pattern of any good college or university in America but that will enable you to do better than such patterns expect you to do.

First, get the habit of shopping around for courses and ideas and professors just as you shop around for dresses or hats, and with as much zest. The world is full of a number of things, and you never know what will turn up at the next counter. Jade Snow Wong is one of America's leading ceramists. In her autobiography, *Fifth Chinese Daughter*, written at the age of twenty-nine (you would enjoy it—and it's been translated into everything from German to Burmese), she tells how she went to college to become a social worker. She vastly enjoyed her studies; but then, in the last semester of her senior year, she took a course in pottery partly because she knew nothing at all about pots. Suddenly, this was it. Today specimens of her work are found in most of the great museum collections of the country. Besides, she has a thriving commercial business, a husband, a couple of button-eyed babies and a life that is almost too full.

One of the best ways to shop around is to get the habit of sitting in, if only for a few lectures or class meetings, on courses in which you are not enrolled. If, one semester, you have a nine o'clock course and an eleven o'clock, take systematic samplings of a few ten o'clock courses. Unless you are a bit of a genius that hour is going to be spent not in studying but in chitchat and having a cup of coffee. At college you will meet many aficionados of the bull session, a cult that believes that to talk—however superficially—about books and ideas and problems is the best possible use of one's time. They are by no means entirely wrong: bulling can be great fun and on occasion intellectually profitable. But you will discover that a good many bull sessions are little more than a pooling of ignorance and of incoherent convictions. So why not take some of your spare-time fun a different way, by sampling classes to get a taste of new academic minds and subjects? Look through the catalogue not only for things that interest you but more particularly for subjects that you are absolutely and dogmatically convinced could never in the world be of the slightest conceivable interest to you. You may get some surprises.

Above all, sample the lectures less of the professors who have a great reputation among your fellow freshmen and the sophs and more of those who are highly regarded among the juniors and seniors majoring in their departments. Many able minds are not particularly articulate, and it is sometimes impossible to find easy and sparkling phrases to fit important ideas. This is especially the case when ideas are really new, just emerging from the cocoon of the mind, just drying their butterfly wings for brilliant flight. Our age is tussling with so many unprecedented ideas that we are having bad vocabulary trouble. While many little minds inflate themselves on stylish gibberish, it is equally true that many great minds are groping to create new verbal symbols with which to handle strange new concepts. This is an exciting time in which to be living and thinking, and the lecture-taster will find that some of the most satisfying and novel dishes are sometimes served in curious forms.

Professors vary in acumen and abilities, as do all other groups of human beings. But you may find that even an apparently dull professor has, hidden deep inside him, a dedication to the truth that is historically descended from the attitudes of the clergy, who first organized the medieval universities and whose priestly regalia of gowns, hoods and mortarboards professors wear on ceremonial occasions. Part of a professor's job is to teach, but an equally important part of his work is to explore the unknown edges of his subject and to think rigorously about it. If he does not teach particularly well, it may still be worth your while to make an effort to find out what it is that has so fascinated him that he has given his life to it.

Once in a somewhat less than thrilling class on the Victorian novel a student asked why the heroines fainted so habitually and was given the conventional reply that they fainted because Victorian ladies wore such tight corsets. The professor thought a moment and then launched into a train of talk that lasted the rest of the lecture hour. Our libraries are filled, he said, with books on the history of architecture and its meanings, yet nobody really knows much about the inwardness of costume. But clothing is a little house that is carried around by people all the time. Like architecture, it gives shelter, it provides beauty and it shows the occupant's status. Because it is seldom "monumental" and soon wears out, it is far less governed by tradition than architecture is, and therefore probably it reflects both the conscious and unconscious needs of the time in a more immediate and intimate way than architecture does. It was one of his ambitions, he said, someday to make sense of the history of dress, but thus far he had failed. At that moment the students felt he had not failed them.

Second in your plan for self-education: I would suggest that you learn to read. America is filled with literate people—indeed, with college graduates—who have never learned to read. To them a book is a task and not an opportunity. They can read a newspaper, a stock report, directions for building a do-it-yourself hi-fi set; but they cannot read anything involving a sequence of ideas. Because of this blind spot in their eyes, they are missing one of the greatest of intellectual satisfactions. And it is a satisfaction that can be deliberately *learned,* just as one can learn to listen to music that has a sequence, development, as distinct from music that is purely episodic.

Sometimes people need help to speed up their reading, but the usual trouble is not knowing how to go about reading. Even if you are planning to read only part of a book, your understanding of it (unless, of course, it is a novel or a play, which must be viewed as an aesthetic whole) will be greatly stepped up if very quickly you can find out why the author has written the book, what his general point of view is and what he thinks he has accomplished. People tend to skip prefaces, and that is a great mistake. By glancing at the preface, the table of contents and the last few paragraphs of the chief chapters—especially of the last chapter—you can very quickly "place" the book, and then you can settle down with some perspective on it to read as much of it as may seem valuable to you. But Harvard's Bureau of Study Counsel observes, in a report on its work with students seeking ways to make their hours of study count, that students seem to feel that this scrutinizing of the conclusion first (a sensible economy, thinks the Bureau) is the moral equivalent of cheating at solitaire. The Counsel's reading class now puts less emphasis on technical aids to faster reading, like the Harvard Reading Films, and tries to discourage compulsive word-for-word reading. The class has begun to be known as "The Right to Think, Even Though Reading."

Naturally, in every course you take in college there will be "readings," either required or suggested. Most students stick to the "required" category, skin through exams and get an education that is therefore skin deep. The "suggested" readings are the beginning of real exploration. If you detect any quiver of curiosity in yourself over something that crops up—how the Vikings built their boats; Fred Hoyle's theory of stellar origins; the contemporary Indonesian dance—then the suggested readings should be just your springboard. One of the notable arguments for going to a college instead of a big university is that colleges let undergraduates prowl the bookstacks of their libraries. From the card catalogue you get the titles and call numbers of a few books relevant to your subject; then, in those wonderful stacks, you find related riches on each side of each book. Our American librarians have made their profession a fine art, and even in the smallest libraries they have developed systems of adjacency for books that show great insight. In big university libraries, where the traffic problem makes it impossible to open the stacks except to professors and graduate students, this same guild of librarians has developed card catalogues to a point of incredible perfection, so that with a little ingenuity one can find all that is useful. And for an undergraduate with real intellectual dynamic, obviously there is more in a university library of a million or more volumes than in an open-stack library of a couple of hundred thousand.

Then there are the guides to periodical literature. If . . . you want to know the latest and hottest stuff on Camus, all you have to do is go to the published indices in the reference department of your library. Not everything will be available, but more than you can possibly read will be at hand. And then if, having eviscerated this material, you go to the professor who knows most about Camus and say, "Dr. Zweibach, I've read such-and-such and such-and-such and such-and-such but don't know where to go from here," he will turn himself inside out to help a student who seems to have generated an authentic intellectual enthusiasm.

Just before I go on to other things, let me remind you that English is not the only civilized tongue. All of you who enter college will have gone through the motions of learning the rudiments of another language, but the idea that anything of the slightest utility or stimulus may have been written in your second language is in danger of eluding you. Let me assure you that, in all the modern tongues you are likely to have studied, Camus and all else have been perceptively discussed, to your great profit if you bother to read the stuff.

Indeed, there are some very important things that you simply can't get in English. To choose random examples: There is no book in our language that gives the insight into the background of European peasant life, and into the formation of the European landscape to be found in Marc Bloch's *Les Caractères originaux de l'histoire rurale francais;* my musical friends tell me that the only work of its kind on the analysis of musical performance is R.M. Haas's *Aufführungspraxis der Musik;* and even as an undergraduate you won't get very far in chemistry without using the German volumes edited by Beilstein. The Tower of Babel is constantly blocking the view of anyone who wants to climb it and get an even wider view from the top.

Item three in your plan of self-education: Why not learn to write? Writing is usually thought of as communication. It is more than that; writing is a means of cerebration. You will remember the story of a philosopher who was asked what he thought about something. "How do I know what I think," he replied, "until I see what I write?" Anyone who writes much knows that the pen or the typewriter is, in the most curious way, an extension of the brain. Having to get the exact words, the *perfect* phrasing for a chain of thought compels us to polish our thinking and remedy its defects. Many a time I have been invited to write or speak on a subject about which my thinking was cloudy. I generally have accepted, because meeting the challenge meant that I would be compelled to clarify my own thinking. For this reason writing can be a joy even though good writing is a great labor.

Professors are usually snowed under with paper work and for this reason seldom ask students to revise essays and reports in the light of criticisms. I would suggest that occasionally, when you know that you could have done a much better job on an assigned paper, you re-do the thing to your own satisfaction and then ask the professor if he won't read the revised version and give it further criticism while letting the original mark stand. This is one of the ways you can develop not only pride in your writing but writing worthy of pride.

Fourth and finally, if you want to become truly educated you should learn the difficult art of listening with what has been called the "third ear." Listening is not just a matter of letting air vibrations impinge upon your nervous system. It involves an act of selfless imagination by which you put yourself into the shoes of the person speaking so that you can know what he is saying even when he isn't quite saying it. Here the thoughtful study of literature, and particularly of the theatre, can be of great help. Most people go through life answering questions that are not being asked and deaf to questions that are being asked. You are probably fortunate [if you are a woman], because the male hormones seem to stimulate an aggressiveness that makes creative listening— a responsiveness less to words than to what lies behind words—very difficult for us men. It is curious how often men are strong on information and women on insight. Yours will not be a complete education until you gain both.

... AND THESE ARE ONLY THE **REQUIRED** READINGS—

CHAPTER 8

How Can You Use the Library Intelligently?

When you learn to use a library you can benefit from the help and advice of the greatest minds of the past and present. But the help they can give you is limited by your own skill in finding it. In this chapter you will find practical suggestions to help you get the maximum benefit from your own college library or from almost any library, since most of them are organized on the same general principles.

VISIT YOUR LIBRARY

You may begin your study of the library by paying it a visit, just to get a general impression of its layout and atmosphere. At this time you can look for the following features, most of which will be explained in the remainder of this chapter:

Card catalog: What classification system is used?

Circulation desk: How are loans recorded?

Reserve collection: Which of your courses have books on reserve?

Reference department: What dictionaries, encyclopedias and atlases are there?

Stacks: Are they open or closed to you?

Periodicals and Newspapers: Where are bound and unbound copies kept?

Vertical files: Are these open or closed?

Special Collections: Does your library have any specialties?

CARD CATALOG

If you will invest a short time now in learning how to use the card catalog, you will save countless hours in the future. Let us begin by examining the outside of the catalog. It consists of a series of drawers in one or more cabinets. On the front of each drawer is a label with an

---

The true university of these days is a collection of books.

Carlyle

---

abbreviation for the first and the last card in that particular drawer. For example, a card for a book written by Margaret Cook might be found in a drawer labeled "Con-De." You will notice that the drawers are arranged vertically in sequence and not horizontally. This arrangement saves the reader many steps when he consults a large catalog. Inside the drawers are several cards for each book in the library, as well as "guide cards" which have tabs that project above the level of the regular catalog cards and describe the contents which follow them.

There are three kinds of cards which are most commonly found in the catalog. By using these cards you can locate a book in the library if you know one of three things about it: who wrote it, what the title is, or what it is about. All books for which an author can be found are listed under the author's name, and most books are listed by title and subject as well. For instance, if you want to use the book, *The New Library Key,* and know that it was written by Margaret G. Cook, you would look in the card catalog under the author's name. Cards for all of the books by Miss Cook will be found together, arranged alphabetically by title.

AUTHOR CARD

```
028.7          —Cook, Margaret G.
C77n              The new library key, 2nd Ed.
                  New York
                  H.W. Wilson, 1963
```

You will notice a number in an upper corner of the card. This is the "**call number**" which tells exactly where on the shelves the book is to be found. It should be remembered that the "author card" is the most important of the several catalog cards for each book because the author card contains complete information about the book.

If you do not know the name of the author, look for the book by title.

TITLE CARD

```
028.7          The new library key
c77n              Cook, Margaret G.
```

Here again, the call number is found on the card and the book can be located easily.

If you know neither the author nor the title of the book you want, you may still be able to find it by looking for a "**subject card**," in this case under the heading LIBRARIES.

SUBJECT CARD

```
                     LIBRARIES
028.7          Cook, Margaret G.
c77n              The new library key
```

SOME AIDS IN USING THE CARD CATALOG

Articles

If the first word of a title is an article (a, an, or the,) look under the next word. *The Mind of the South* is filed under "mind": *A Treasury of the Theater* is filed under "treasury."

Abbreviations

Abbreviations are filed as though they were spelled out: "Dr." as "Doctor," "Mrs." as "Mistress," "U.S." as "United States" and "St." as "Saint."

Numerals

Numerals are filed as though they were spelled out. *101 Plots Used and Abused* is filed under "One-hundred-one."

Mac and Mc

Names beginning with Mc and Mac are filed as though they were spelled Mac, as follows:

> Mackay
> McKay
> MacKaye
> McKean

De, Van, or Von

When these particles are parts of English names and are capitalized, the filing is according to the entire word.

Word by word

When several words begin with the same letters, the shorter words are filed before the longer words:

log	Newark
logarithm	newspaper editing
moral	newspaper waste
morale	Newspapers in a democracy
new age	Newspapers in the country
New Orleans	newt
New York	Newton

Author cards and subject cards

Cards for books *by* an author are filed before cards *about* an author. In other words, author cards come *before* subject cards.

AUTHOR CARD COMES FIRST

SUBJECT CARD FOLLOWS

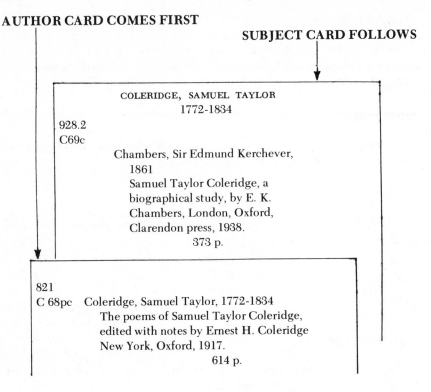

OTHER CATALOG CARDS

"See" cards

"See" reference cards are used to direct you from alternative or synonymous words which are *not* used, to the terms which are used.

> Domestic Science
> see
> Home Economics

If you cannot find the subject you are looking for, always try to think of alternative ways of saying the same thing. Eventually, you will either get directly to your subject or else to a "see" or "see also" card.

"See also" cards

These cards suggest headings you should look under for related or additional material on a given subject. For example, at the end of the file of subject cards on reading, you may find a card which reads as follows:

```
┌─────────────────────────────────────────────────┐
│         Reading                                   │
│           see also                                │
│         Diction                                   │
│         Elocution                                 │
│         Readers and speakers                      │
│                                                   │
└─────────────────────────────────────────────────┘
```

Another very useful way to find additional or related material is to use suggestions at the bottom of the regular catalog cards.

```
┌─────────────────────────────────────────────────┐
│   028.7                                           │
│   c77n.     Cook, Margaret Gerry, 1903-           │
│             The new library key, 2nd Ed., New York, Wilson, │
│                                                   │
│         1.  Reference books.  2.  Books and reading │
│                                                   │
└─────────────────────────────────────────────────┘
```

Thus, if you can find in the card catalog one book on a subject of interest, you can often find at the bottom of the card subject headings that will lead to additional material.

Analytics

Cards for parts of books are called "analytics" and may be author, title, or subject cards. Essays, plays, short stories, and biographies are often located through these cards. Just be certain to copy the complete call number correctly so you can obtain the book.

LIBRARIANS

In most libraries the most valuable single resource is the librarian. But, just as with other resources, it is best to use him or her conservatively. That is, do not ask a librarian for assistance until you have made an honest effort to find the information yourself. There are several reasons for this. In the first place, the search itself can be very educational for you. Second, it sometimes takes a long time to explain just what you want. Third, a college librarian sometimes feels that college students ought to be able to use a card catalog before they send out the distress signal.

CLASSIFICATION SYSTEMS

It is perfectly possible to use the card catalog and obtain books by using their call numbers without understanding the classification system which is the source of the call numbers. All you have to do is copy the number from the catalog card and the book you want can be located. Nevertheless, it is often very useful to understand how your library has classified its books. Most college libraries, except the very largest, use the Dewey Decimal Classification developed by Melvil Dewey about 1876. In this system, all books are placed in ten general categories which are then further subdivided. A few examples follow:

000 General works (encyclopedias, bibliographies, periodicals)
      030 General Encyclopedias
      070 Journalism

100 Philosophy and Psychology
      150 Psychology

200 Religions
      220 Bible

300 Social Sciences
      310 Statistics
      320 Political Science
      330 Economics
      340 Law
      370 Education
      380 Commerce

400 Languages (Philology)
      420 English language
      430 German
      440 French

500 Sciences ("Pure" Science)
      510 Mathematics
      520 Astronomy
      530 Physics
      540 Chemistry
      550 Earth sciences
      570 Biological sciences
      580 Botany
      590 Zoology

600 Applied Sciences (Useful Arts)
      610 Medicine
      620 Engineering

630 Agriculture
650 Business and business methods

700 Fine Arts and Recreation
720 Architecture
780 Music
790 Recreation

800 Literature
810 American literature
820 English literature

900 History, geography, biography
910 Geography
920 Biography

If necessary, each of these categories can be divided more finely, first by enlarging the third digit and later by adding decimal places. Thus, 800 is Literature; 820 is English literature; 822 is English Drama; 822.3 is Elizabethan Drama; and 822.33 is Shakespeare.

With the knowledge of what the call numbers stand for, a student should be able to go to the shelves and preview a subject field before selecting the appropriate book. In looking for books on the shelves, keep in mind that decimal numbers follow one another in a progression different from whole numbers:

WHOLE NUMBERS—2, 9, 11, 15, 73
DECIMALS—.11, .15, .2, .73, .9

Many libraries use another numbering system in addition to the Dewey Classification. This provides the "Cutter number," based on the author's name and the book title. It is placed below the Dewey number. The Dewey and Cutter numbers together make up the usual "call number." Often a library will add a letter above these numbers to give further information. Thus, "R" means reference and "B" means biography. Be sure to include all such letters and numbers when copying the call number.

Library of Congress Classification

Many of the largest university libraries use the Library of Congress Classification which is similar to the Dewey but which provides somewhat shorter call numbers. The major categories of this system follow:

A   General Works
B   Philosophy and Religion
C—D   History and Auxiliary Sciences, Excluding America

E—F   America
G   Geography and Anthropology
H   Social Sciences
J   Political Science
K   Law
L   Education
M   Music
N   Fine Arts
P   Language and Literature
Q   Science
R   Medicine
S   Agriculture
T   Technology
U   Military Science
V   Naval Science
Z   Bibliography and Library Science

PERIODICAL INDEXES

Periodicals such as newspapers and magazines are storehouses of up-to-date material on every imaginable subject. The keys that unlock these storehouses are the periodical indexes, which are described below.

Reader's Guide to Periodical Literature (1900 to date). This is the best known and most widely used of the indexes. It covers well over one hundred magazines of general interest ranging from *American Artist* to the *Yale Review* and including *Better Homes and Gardens, Harper's, Life, Mademoiselle, New York Times Magazine, Plays, Poetry,* and the *Scientific American.* An explanation of the abbreviations used is found inside the cover of each issue. The *Reader's Guide* appears about every two weeks and there are cumulative issues monthly, every few months, annually and biennially. For references to English and American periodicals prior to 1900, consult *Poole's Index.*

New York Times Index (1913 to date). Published semi-monthly, with annual cumulations, this index serves as a detailed authoritative record of current events and as a guide to other newspapers besides the *New York Times.* That is, you can find stories in other newspapers either by getting the date from the *Times Index* or perhaps because the *Times* article mentions the paper in which you are interested.

Other more specialized indexes to periodicals which are found in many college libraries include:

Agricultural Index
Art Index
Bibliographic Index
Biography Index
Education Index
Engineering Index
Essay and General Literature Index
Facts on File
Industrial Arts Index
International Index: a Quarterly Guide to Periodical Literature in the Social Sciences and Humanities.

Some hints on the use of periodical indexes

To get the latest information on any subject, begin with the latest paper-bound number of the index and work back systematically. For material on a subject connected with a certain period of time, you ordinarily need consult only the index covering this period.

BOOK REVIEWS

Often it is very helpful to read a critical opinion or review of a book one has used or expects to use. Many such comments can be found in the *Book Review Digest* (1905 to date), which is published monthly with annual cumulations, the index being cumulated every five years.

Another publication helpful to college students is the *Technical Book Review Index* (1917 to date), which is similar to the *Book Review Digest* but concentrates on scientific and technical books. You may find it amusing and instructive to see what has been said by experts about the textbooks you are using.

REFERENCE BOOKS

Dictionaries

You are accustomed to using a dictionary to verify the spelling, meaning, and pronunciation of words. The big unabridged dictionaries contain this information and much more besides. As a college student, you should make a habit of using several dictionaries instead of relying on any one. The following two encyclopedic dictionaries are most important:

Webster's New International Dictionary has definitions arranged in historical order. The most modern meaning of the word is *last*. Uncommon words and foreign phrases are below the line on each page of the Second Edition. Both Second and Third Editions are in current use.

Funk and Wagnall's New Standard Dictionary has definitions arranged with the most modern meaning *first*. Foreign words are in an appendix.

Be sure to examine the *New English Dictionary on Historical Principles* (Oxford, 1888-1933), also known as the Oxford English Dictionary, OED, or NED. This gives the history of almost every word used in England from 1150 to 1933, doing it in a mere ten volumes, plus a supplement.

Encyclopedias

Unlike dictionaries, which give definitions of words, encyclopedias attempt to give comprehensive studies of selected topics, and to furnish bibliographical leads to further information. These works vary greatly in size, from the one-volume *Columbia-Viking Desk Encyclopedia* to the two major encyclopedias, the *Americana,* in thirty volumes, and the *Britannica,* in twenty-four.° There are also many specialized encyclopedias which may be available in your library. As one example, the *Encyclopedia of the Social Sciences* is particularly valuable, both for its articles and its bibliographies.

One big problem with encyclopedias is that many articles become out-of-date almost as soon as they are written. Because of this, the better encyclopedias provide yearbooks or supplements.

On occasion, you may want to make use of encyclopedias intended for children and young people, but which are useful for your first approach to a technical subject. For example, the *World Book* is rated as exceptionally helpful for explaining scientific subjects and the *Britannica Junior* contains particularly clear introductions to mathematical topics.

OTHER REFERENCES

In the reference section of your library you will find various books and other resources leading you to almost any kind of information. Be-

---

°As an antidote to overreliance on an encyclopedia, see Harvey Einbinder, *The Myth of the Britannica,* (New York: Grove Press, 1964), although most of the criticisms were corrected in later printings of the **Britannica.**

come acquainted with these valuable research aids so that you can have them at your service when you need them:

Almanac—annual compendium of brief facts and statistics. Example: *World Almanac.*

Atlas—collection of maps or plates. Example: *Shepherd's Historical Atlas.*

Bibliography—list of writings relating to a given subject, period, or author. Example: *Cambridge Bibliography of English Literature.*

Biographical dictionary—dictionary of names of noteworthy persons with brief biographical sketches. Example: *Who's Who in America.*

Concordance—alphabetical list of the leading words, phrases or topics in a book showing their location, often in their exact context. Example: *Cruden's Complete Concordance to the Old and New Testaments.*

Directory—alphabetical or classified list of persons or organizations, with identifying information. Example: *American Colleges and Universities.*

Gazetteer—geographical dictionary. Example: *Lippincott's Complete Pronouncing Gazetteer.*

Handbook—book of miscellaneous information on one or several subjects compiled for quick reference. Example: *Oxford Companion to American Literature.*

Pamphlet—publication consisting of a few printed sheets, generally in paper covers, that can be valuable for timeliness.

Quotation book—handbook that quotes and cites the location of statements by a given author, or on a given subject. Example: *Bartlett's Familiar Quotations.*

Statistical handbook—collection of statistical information giving sources. Example: *Statistical Abstract of the United States.*

Style manual—handbook that defines and illustrates accepted usages and bibliographic forms. Example: University of Chicago, *A Manual of Style.*

Thesaurus—collection of words of similar meanings arranged according to the ideas they express. Example: *Roget's Thesaurus.*

Vertical file—collection of pamphlets, clippings, pictures, etc., generally kept in filing cabinets and arranged alphabetically by subject.

Yearbook—annual of current information. Example: *Britannica Book of the Year.*

VIEWPOINT

Building Your Own Basic Library
BY J. SHERWOOD WEBER

Everyone ... [should] ... equip his desk shelf with volumes that will answer most of his questions much of the time. Thanks to the paperbound explosion, even a student can afford a serviceable small collection of general and personal reference books.

                                    o   o   o

The first absolute "must" for anyone's desk library is a good dictionary. Unfortunately, any dictionary is not a good dictionary: if it is small, it omits too much; if it is not younger than a decade, it is too dated; if it lacks a sturdy cover, tough paper and sound binding, it will dog-ear and disintegrate. For one or more of these reasons, any paperbound dictionary, though useful, is inadequate. Every student should therefore possess one of these four hardcover standard abridged dictionaries: *The American College Dictionary* (Random House); *Standard College Dictionary* (Funk & Wagnalls, and Harcourt, Brace & World); *Webster's New World Dictionary, College Edition* (World); *Webster's Seventh New Collegiate Dictionary* (Merriam). Only one of these, the *New World*, is published in paperback as well. The saving is not worth the inconvenience.

All of these dictionaries are very good, yet all differ significantly from each other—in their orders of listing definitions or in their "extras." Before purchasing any one, the student should examine all four, read their prefaces, and choose the one with which he feels most comfortable. He cannot choose poorly. He should realize, however, that it takes time and effort to learn how to use any dictionary effectively; few know how, because few take this time.

Smaller paperbound dictionaries have their uses too, but not on the desk reference shelf. Every student can profit from, and probably afford, several paperbound dictionaries; one for armchair or bed reading, one for briefcase or bookbag, one for glove compartment or locker. These can serve for quick consultation when and where the bulkier superior dictionaries are inconvenient to carry and use. Among the better less-than-$1 paperbounds are *New American Webster Handy College Dictionary* (New American Library), *New Merriam-Webster Pocket Dictionary* (Pocket Books) and *Thorndike-Barnhart Handy Dictionary* (Bantam).

Closely allied to general dictionaries, and somewhat duplicating the resources

---

°Abstracted by permission from J. Sherwood Weber, "Helping the Student to Find It," *New York Times Book Review* (January 10, 1965), pp. 20-21. © 1965 by The New York Times Company. Reprinted by permission.

of any of the four cloth-covered leaders cited above, are books of synonyms and antonyms and words of current usage. Any writer who desires to locate the best word to communicate his meaning will want to own one or more of the following: *New American Roget's College Thesaurus in Dictionary Form* (New American Library), *Roget's New Pocket Thesaurus in Dictionary Form* (Washington Square), *Soule's Dictionary of English Synonyms* (Bantam), or *Dictionary of American-English Usage* (New American Library).

Any student with more-than-passing interest in a specific subject area will find under the "Reference Book" listings of the latest cumulative *Paperbound Books in Print* special dictionaries for almost any discipline. Before buying any, visit a large bookstore to examine and weigh the competition. Determining the best general and specialized dictionaries for one's personal use cannot proceed by rule of thumb. Examination, then choice, must follow the advice given above.

When we shift attention from general dictionaries to general encyclopedias, we move from multiplicity and confusion to crystal-clear clarity. Without a doubt the... [best]... is the *Columbia-Viking Desk Encyclopedia* (Dell). Unless the student can afford *The Columbia Encyclopedia* [itself], he cannot afford to do without its abridged, big little-brother. Its one volume of 2,016 pages comprises 31,700 entries plus assorted maps, tables and drawings. The type is small but readable, and the material is sound, diverse, up-to-date. Any reader will consult it often and generally find what he wants.

Another requirement for every student reference collection is a good fact book. *The World Almanac and Book of Facts* (brought up to date and published each year by... [various regional newspapers]), though helter-skelter in its organization, contains a mine of recent data on a wide variety of subjects and a thorough index to guide the user to the lodes. I never cease being astonished at what I can find in it. Any serious citizen should buy a new edition at least every two years.

Our one world—geographically and communicatively if not politically and socially—demands that every student posses a world atlas. Paperbound atlases are often good, though anyone who uses them often (large atlases are rather expensive) will also want to own a small magnifying glass. Again I suggest examining the competing items before buying one. Among the world atlases meriting attention are *Barnes and Noble World Atlas* (Barnes & Noble), *New Hammond-Dell World Atlas* (Dell), *New Hammond World Atlas* (Bantam) and *New Rand McNally Pocket World Atlas* (Pocket Books).

For writing essays on almost any subject and for preparing speeches (including debates), the student will often find valuable a book of quotations. Among the more useful of these are *The Shorter Bartlett's Familiar Quotations* (Pocket Books), *Best Quotations for all Occasions* (Fawcett-Premier) and *Popular Quotations for all Uses* (Doubleday-Dolphin).

The final general reference book of appeal to all students—high school, college, or self-directed—is a bibliographical guide to reading in all subjects. *Good Reading* (New American Library) lists about 2,000 first-rate books of all historical periods, all literary types and all humanities, social sciences and sciences; briefly describes each, including its level of difficulty; and cites most editions in print, with emphasis on paper-bounds.

Other annotated reading lists of this kind are narrower in scope. *The College and Adult Reading List* (Washington Square) focuses on books in literature and the fine arts, giving detailed, almost page-long summaries and analyses; and *A Guide to Science Reading* (New American Library) describes science books for all levels.

Every workable college student desk reference collection will contain at least one volume from each category discussed. Of course, a good personal reference library will include additional volumes, depending on the individual's subject specialties, age, hobbies and reading preferences.

                                   o   o   o

The additional reference books of the college student will be dictated by his subject major and his extra-curricular interests. If he majors in language or literature he should not miss *The Reader's Companion to World Literature* (New American Library), a specialized encyclopedia of authors, titles, plots, literary movements and genres, historical periods and literary terms. If his specialty is history, he will certainly find useful *Dictionary of Modern History* (Penguin). If he is studying a foreign language he will need a dictionary of that language. The key thing to remember is this: what you want probably exists in a paper-bound edition.

CHAPTER 9

How Should You Study the Humanities?

Almost every student will concede that one of his purposes in attending college is to become an educated person. When you ask him to explain what he means by this he may answer that he wants to understand the world better, to understand other human beings and himself, and to develop new and wider interests and appreciations, all of which he feels are the marks of a truly educated man. Yet, strangely enough, the student often resists the very courses designed to help him attain these goals. Some avoid classical music, scoff at poetry, and shun any serious reading. And the reason they give for avoiding these new experiences is that they have never enjoyed them before.

The humanities are often feared because they require an intense degree of personal involvement. But in return they offer you a clearer understanding of yourself as you widen your range of experiences. The humanities can give you a deeper appreciation of other people and other cultures as you study the books and the arts they create and enjoy. Humanities are also valuable for making college courses meaningful. As only one example, psychological principles come alive in literature just as literature is illuminated by a knowledge of psychology.

As knowledge becomes more fragmented into the various specialties, it becomes essential that all educated people possess common experiences so that they can continue to communicate with each other. The humanities are the foundation of these necessary common experiences.

In previous chapters you learned some general techniques for studying any college course. Now you will examine the special goals, problems, and methods of studying particular subjects.

> *No one can become really educated without having pursued some study in which he took no interest—for it is part of education to learn to interest ourselves in subjects for which we have no aptitude.*
>
> T. S. Eliot

In my opinion college is much to [sic] easy.

From a freshman essay

What is most needed for learning is a humble mind.

Confucius

LEARNING ENGLISH COMPOSITION

Why study English composition?

According to undergraduate folklore, every college instructor secretly feels that his own subject is the most important one in the entire curriculum. Yet, almost any instructor might concede that the study of the English language is just about as important as his own specialty. The reason for this is not hard to find, for the essence of all education is the communication of ideas, and English is the primary means by which we communicate. Consequently, almost every college expects its entering students to take at least a year of English composition and rhetoric (1). Often, a freshman has developed the ability to express himself clearly and accurately before he entered college. Composition classes then serve mainly to polish and expand the skills he has brought with him. The English Department would like the student to go beyond mere competence and tries to develop in each student a distinctive and appropriate style. Unfortunately, many students today enter college without the elementary skill of writing clear and accurate English. It is these students who furnish a majority of the failures in the first year of college.

I have a problem in english it was hard for me when I was in grammar school through high school and now in college.
From a freshman essay

One of your first concerns in college should be to find out whether or not you have any serious deficiencies in the skills of reading and writing. If your entrance test or self-test shows that your basic skills are adequate, you will need to devote only as much attention to English composition as you would to any other major subject. But if you find that you lack these skills, no other course you take will be as essential for your success in college. In particular, you must be able to read with speed and comprehension. If you have doubts about this, it would be prudent for you to take as light a course load as possible until you are certain that your reading and writing abilities are up to standard. There are two advantages in reducing your work load, if it becomes necessary: first, you will gain study time to devote to English; and second, you will postpone some subjects until you are able to deal with them more efficiently.

Reading and understanding has been my main problem. If and when I can do that well I think college will be a lot eassyer [*sic*].
From a freshman essay

Good writing

Keep in mind that *the purpose of writing is communication* between the writer and the reader. **Grammatical errors** or any other errors block the transmission of ideas no matter how brilliant these may be. Even if the reader can decipher the meaning you intended, the extra effort he has to put forth may make him less willing to accept what you are trying to say. Certain common errors in composition can be summarized in a few pages of your textbook, yet they furnish the bulk of mistakes found in college student writing.

A good style must first of all be clear. It must be neither below nor above the dignity of the subject. It must be appropriate.

Aristotle

Among other essentials, good writing requires **careful organization of ideas and the precise choice of words.** Speaking comes before writing. When you find it difficult to write what you mean, try to explain it out loud. You may then be able to write more easily. To help with your choice of words, have a copy of *Roget's Thesaurus* handy when you write, but do not use it just to find difficult or obscure terms, as some do. Instead, use it for finding the exact word you need.

Errors in spelling also handicap your writing. English is said to be the only major language in which educated persons commonly make mistakes in spelling. This may be due to the inherent difficulties of a language drawn from numerous sources and one which has undergone many rapid changes. Still, you will find it necessary to learn to spell common words correctly. For your convenience, a list of words most often misspelled by college freshman has been added at the end of this chapter. In addition to memorizing this list, you will benefit from learning the few rules of spelling which are also supplied.

The best answer to the problem of spelling is to **develop the habit** of always giving it your careful attention. When you find an unfamiliar word, learn to pronounce it, to divide it correctly, and to use it accurately. Always keep a dictionary nearby when you write, and look up every single word that raises a doubt in your mind. After a while, you should find that there are fewer words for you to look up, and you will also find that the level of your writing has improved.

English orthography satisfies all the requirements of the canons of respectability under the law of conspicuous waste. It is archaic, cumbrous, and ineffective; its acquisition consumes much time and effort; failure to acquire it is easy of detection.

Thorstein Veblen

LEARNING SPEECH

Speech is civilization itself. The word, even the most contradictory word, preserves contact—it is silence which isolates.

Thomas Mann

Today, many colleges either require speech as a separate subject or include it as part of a required course in communications; it is certainly one of the most important of the communication skills. Speech is used in every person's life for conversation. In teaching it is used for exposition and for lecturing. In religion it is used for spiritual guidance. In selling it is used for persuasion. In law it is used for argument. In all professions it plays a major role in influencing the behavior of listeners.

The primary purpose of speech courses is to improve your skill in oral communication. Modern speaking style tries to retain the most desirable elements of informal conversation—ease, spontaneity, intimacy. Thus a good speech should not be written, or read, or memorized. Rather, it should be carefully thought, planned, and outlined.

Frequently, the college freshman enters a speech class with a false idea of what speech is; and many students, particularly the brightest, suffer seriously from stage fright. Nevertheless, virtually all freshmen complete their first speech course with the feeling that they have enjoyed the class and derived great benefit from it.

APPRECIATION AND ENJOYMENT OF LITERATURE

Literature is not an abstract science, to which exact definitions can be applied. It is an art, the success of which depends on personal persuasiveness, on the author's skill to give as on ours to receive.
Sir Arthur Quiller-Couch

Why study literature?

The number of books in the world today is overwhelming—tens of millions of them: fiction, non-fiction, poetry, drama. How can you choose those which will be useful and enjoyable to you? How can you avoid wasting time on the dull and worthless ones? To help you to become sensitive to the differences between good and bad writing and to form sound standards of judgment for choosing your own future reading are major objectives of your course in literature. In class you will be presented with a number of examples of literature to read carefully, discuss, and evaluate. Some of them you may appreciate immediately, some of them later, and some never. More important, though, you will be awakened to new ideas, experiences, attitudes, and feelings. With a broadening of the range of literature you can enjoy, there may come an expansion of yourself as a human being.

In addition to helping you formulate standards for your future reading, there are other objectives for college courses in literature, and other benefits you may derive. Your instructor will undoubtedly make clear which of these have been chosen for your course, but keep in mind that there are few courses which have a greater potentiality for changing your life.

How should prose literature be studied?

Your instructor in literature, more so than your other instructors, will be interested in just how you study his subject. He will have some specific and useful recommendations for you which you would be well advised to follow exactly. A few general suggestions, however, may be of some value here.

First, a good deal depends upon the *attitude* with which you approach your readings. Some students expect to appreciate and enjoy great literature—and they are rarely disappointed. They are in the position of those fortunate individuals who have jobs in which they are paid for doing just what they would be doing anyhow. Other students anticipate that their literature course will be deadly dull and, while a few are pleasantly surprised, some find their fears are realized, perhaps largely because of their own prejudices. Mark Twain reflected this viewpoint when he remarked, "A classic is something that everyone wants to have read and nobody wants to read."

When studying literature you must use a *technique* different from that used for other subjects, for the writer of imaginative literature proceeds not so much by direct statement as by implication and suggestion. You must learn to respond to his hints and clues. Ask yourself why the author included a particular detail or description. What does it reveal about the character or the action which is described? There are many other details the author might have mentioned instead, but he has chosen to omit them. What the author has included thus represents his decision as to what is important for creating a dramatic picture of the truth as he sees it. You as the reader must always be alert to respond to the implications of the author's statements.

Be sure to **allow yourself enough time** to do justice to your readings. Your assignments should be carefully read more than once, with as much time between readings as possible, for literature ripens in the mind and this process takes time. Readers are often surprised at how much more they understand when they go over a selection again and again. Inexperienced students often underestimate how much time the readings will require and do not start their assignments until it is too late. To see someone beginning *Moby Dick* the night before the final examination is truly a pitiful sight.

Literature, like every other college subject, has its own vocabulary. This vocabulary seems particularly rich in words which the student has heard before but is unable to define very precisely. In order to master literary criticism, the student must learn to use its technical terms with ease and accuracy.

How should poetry be studied?

"Poetry," said Matthew Arnold, "is simply the most beautiful, impressive, and widely effective mode of saying things, and hence its importance." You will find poetry to be at once the most enjoyable and the most complex of the arts. Essentially, it consists of taking a great deal of meaning and compressing it into a uniquely memorable form. While prose literature usually is written on a single level of meaning, poetry may have many meanings combined for maximum impact and emotional appeal. When you read poetry you should, therefore, look not only for meaning but for the poetic effect upon yourself. Incidentally, it is not necessary for poetry to rhyme, nor is it true that because a verse is rhymed it must be poetry.

As you start the serious study of poetry, you will have several sources of help and guidance: the editor's introduction to an anthology of poems; any of several excellent general guides to poetry which your instructor may recommend; and, most important of all, your instructor himself. We, too, have a few suggestions which you may find useful.

Begin your study of a poem by **reading it aloud,** enjoying its rhythm, melody, and story. Perhaps you will find that your own experiences or emotions are reflected in the poem, or perhaps the poem will take you into a strange and remote world. In either case, try to **appreciate your own special relationship** to the poem. Next, **look for the hidden meanings and symbolism** which may be present. This search is most difficult when you first begin to study poetry and are not yet familiar with the sources used by the poet. The more you read poetry, the more you will find yourself equipped to deal with symbolism and allusion. Finally, **study the poem for its rhythmic system and rhyme-pattern** if it has one. Here again, this process will become easier as you read more poetry and are better able to make comparisons and contrasts among many different poems.

Above all, try to **appreciate poetry as an unusual emotional and intellectual adventure.** As Robert Frost wrote:

> **Two roads diverged in a wood, and I—**
> **I took the one less traveled by,**
> **And that has made all the difference.**°

°From "The Road Not Taken," from *Complete Poems of Robert Frost*. Copyright 1916, 1921 by Holt, Rinehart and Winston, Inc. Copyright renewed 1944 by Robert Frost. Reprinted by permission of Holt, Rinehart and Winston, Inc.

LEARNING FOREIGN LANGUAGES

A man is worth as many men as he knows languages.
Ascribed to Charles V

Growing importance of foreign languages

Interest in the study of foreign languages has increased tremendously in recent years. As a result of the changing world situation many people have come to believe that we may not be able to survive unless we learn to communicate with other peoples. One effect of this interest has been that, since 1958, the government has been actively encouraging the study of various languages. More colleges now require a foreign language and more students choose to take additional work beyond the minimum requirements.

The whole field of teaching and learning languages is being transformed at the present time. There is much greater stress on *communication instead of on the translation* of great works of literature. Skill in reading and writing is now often built upon previous training in listening and speaking. A variety of techniques are employed; among them, audio-lingual laboratories, sequenced learning devices, and special intensive courses. Another recent development is a great interest in such major languages as Russian, Japanese, and Mandarin-Chinese, which were previously neglected by most American schools.

For you as a student, these developments mean that the ability to communicate in another language may become one of the major benefits of your college experience. Many vocational opportunities—in industry, commerce, education, and government service—both in this country and abroad, are open for those who have some degree of ability in another language. Moreover, the ability to use at least one foreign language has long been regarded as a necessity for a truly cultured individual. As Goethe remarked, unless you know a foreign language, you cannot truly understand your own.

How to study

Despite all the new techniques, learning a langauge is still a difficult and time-consuming process, and it is well to face the problem realistically. Let us consider three factors involved in learning a language: motivation, aptitude, and background. Of these three, your *motivation* or the strength of your desire to learn is probably the most important. If you want to learn the language, and if you apply yourself correctly, you can do it, in almost every instance. The second factor is your *natural aptitude* for language as shown on one of the standard tests. This test should give some indication of how much effort it will take for you to succeed; but a high language aptitude does not guarantee success, nor does a low aptitude doom you to failure. The third factor in learning a language is the *linguistic background* with which you enter the course. Generally speaking, the greater the familiarity you have with the structure of English and the greater your knowledge of any other language, the easier it will be for you to learn still more, provided that you do not expect the new language to follow the same rules as the languages you already know.

College language courses have differing objectives. Some stress reading and translation; others stress listening, comprehension, and speaking. Your instructor will emphasize the techniques most appropriate to the aims of the course. Your textbook will also have some suggestions for studying the language and you will find it profitable to follow them.

Whatever techniques you use for studying, it is absolutely essential that you keep up with your class work **every single day,** as each lesson builds upon the previous one. In addition, it is your responsibility to keep previous work fresh in your mind by means of regular and systematic reviewing, for it will require an enormous amount of repeated practice before your language habits will become automatic and thus usable when you need them. As a great linguist, Leonard Bloomfield, wrote, "Language learning is overlearning; anything less is of no use."

Methods of learning vocabulary

It is often suggested that language students make use of *vocabulary cards.* These are small cards or slips of paper, each of which has a word in the foreign language written on one side and its English equivalent on the other. You may be able to purchase such cards already printed, or else you may prefer to make your own. Making your own cards is time-consuming but useful as a means of learning. The cards or slips are used in this way: A student selects about fifty cards at a time. He begins by studying both sides of each card and later runs through them again looking at only one side, as a test. Word cards that he identifies correctly are put to one side and the words he misses are restudied. Vocabulary cards are especially convenient when carried in the pocket or purse for studying at odd moments which would otherwise be wasted.

Another technique for studying the vocabulary of some languages is to watch carefully for *cognate words* in your readings. By this we mean words in foreign language which resemble English words. The English language, derived for the most part from a Germanic source and a Romance source, has many "root words" in common with various European languages. Be careful when you use cognates because words undergo shifts of meaning as time passes. For example, the French word *conférence* (English "lecture") has a very different meaning from its English cognate, "conference."

The learning of vocabulary can also be facilitated if you **analyze complex words** so that you can remember their constituent parts, which may appear in other words. A simple example in English is the word "midshipman," made up of three constituent parts, each of which has a meaning of its own. Note, however, that the complete word has a meaning different from the sum of the three parts.

By far the best method of learning vocabulary is to learn each word *in the context* of many different sentences, which, of course, is the natural way children learn their own language.

Methods of learning grammar

Every language has its own structure patterns which are commonly called its grammar. The ability to use any language requires above all else a thorough mastery of its grammatical patterns. You will find it a great timesaver to learn the rules, not only well enough for repetition on an examination, but well enough so their use becomes automatic for you.

One major obstacle to learning the grammar of a foreign language is that many college students have only a fragmentary knowledge of English grammar. If this is a problem for you, be sure to write down every grammatical term your instructor uses and later look it up in the dictionary or in a language textbook to make certain that you understand it. Among the traditional grammatical terms are: *noun, verb, adjective, adverb, direct object, indirect object, gender, person, number, case, declension, conjugation, tense, mood, voice.* Unless you understand the correct usage of all these terms, you will be at a serious disadvantage in most language courses.

Every language contains its own idioms or peculiar usages which cannot be translated literally. As a matter of fact, the English language itself is rich in idioms, as the following examples will illustrate:

> *On your own*
> *How do you do?*
> *Drop in . . . drop by*
> *Get in touch with someone*

All you can do with idioms is to accept them and memorize them.

Do not get discouraged when you find that the language you are studying has many "exceptions" to the rules you have memorized (2). Just remember that the rules came after the language had developed and they are merely attempts at general statements which will describe usage. Normally, a language has a tremendous amount of regularity, but do not expect a language to show more consistency then anything else which is man-made.

Some instructors prefer that you learn grammar mainly by repeating word patterns used in communicating. In any event, transitive verbs should always be conjugated with both a subject and a direct object. An English example would be *not* merely "throw, threw, thrown" but rather,

> I throw a ball now.
> I threw a ball yesterday.
> I have thrown a ball in the past.

If they are available, you will also find it helpful to read newspapers, magazines, or books in the foreign language, perhaps starting with illustrated children's books. Newspapers are particularly valuable because they usually represent current usage in the language. Moreover, they deal with matters with which you should already have some familiarity.

Learning to speak a foreign language

The most important suggestion for learning a language is that you use it as much as possible, even if you have to talk to yourself. Speak it. Read it. Write it. Do not be afraid of making mistakes. There is supposed to be a Bulgarian proverb which warns, "In order to master a language, you must first murder it!"

Many of the sounds in a foreign language are quite different from their related sounds in English. For this reason it is desirable that, whenever possible, you listen to native speakers, attend foreign language motion pictures, and use the language recordings which your instructor may recommend. You should learn to imitate these as closely as possible, paying attention to intonation and accent as well as to the vowels and consonants. This will take repeated practice and drill.

It is best to do your studying out loud. It is also helpful to use a tape recorder so that you too can criticize your efforts. Above all, in both your speech and your writing, strive for an authentic native style. Try to **think in the language,** if possible, without having to translate from English. When you can do this you will have mastered the language.

One Hundred Words Most Frequently Misspelled
by College Freshmen

ARRANGED IN ORDER OF FREQUENCY *

their	definite	description	personal
they're	definitely	describe	personnel
there	definition		
	define	benefit	than
too		benefited	then
two	separate	beneficial	
to	separation		principle
		precede	principal
receive	believe	referring	
receiving	belief		choose
		success	chose
	occasion	succeed	choice
exist		succession	
existence			
existent	lose	its	perform
	losing	it's	performance
occur			similar
occurred	write	privilege	
occurring	writing		professor
occurrence	writer	environment	profession
necessary	tries	realize	passed
unnecessary	tried	really	past
began	weather	led	acquire
begin	whether		
beginner		loneliness	busy
beginning	forty	lonely	business
	fourth		
control		prefer	Negro
controlled	criticism	preferred	Negroes
controlling	criticize		
		surprise	among

°Thomas Clark Pollock, "Spelling Report." *College English* (November, 1954), based on 31,375 misspellings in college themes found by 600 English teachers in 52 colleges in 27 states. Reprinted with the permission of the National Council of Teachers of English and Professor Thomas Clark Pollock.

One Hundred Words Most Frequently Misspelled
by College Freshmen (Continued)

argument	apparent		
arguing		explanation	height
	sense		
proceed		fascinate	interest
procedure	conscious		
		immediate	origin
achieve	studying	immediately	original
achievement			
	varies	interpretation	conscience
controversy	various	interpret	conscientious
controversial			
	category	thorough	accommodate
all right			
	embarrass	useful	comparative
psychology	embarrassment	useless	
psychoanalysis		using	decision
psychopathic	excellent		decided
psychosomatic	excellence	noticeable	
		noticing	experience
possess	grammar		
possession	grammatically	probably	
			prominent
analyze	repetition	imagine	
analysis		imaginary	pursue
		imagination	
equipped	consistent		
equipment	consistency		shining
		marriage	
affect	prevalent		
affective		prejudice	
	intelligence		
rhythm	intelligent	disastrous	

Some Spelling Rules
Based on the One Hundred Words Most
Frequently Misspelled

1. Be sure to **pronounce** the word correctly, paying special attention to the unstressed sounds.
   Examples: existence, separate, description, benefit, environment, than, then, perform, similar, affect, effect.

2. For words ending in silent "**e**" (except those ending in "**ce**" or "**ge**"), drop the "**e**" before a suffix beginning with a vowel.

Keep the "e" before a suffix beginning with a consonant.
Examples: achieve, achieving, achievement; write, writing, writer; use, using, useful.
Exceptions: ninth, truly, wholly.

3. For words ending in "ce" or "ge."
Keep the "e" before the suffix (unless the suffix begins with "e" or "i").
Drop the "e" before a suffix beginning with "e" or "i".
Examples: notice, noticeable, noticing; manage, management, manager; courage, courageous.
Exception: judgment.

4. "I" comes before "e" except after "c," or when sounded like "a," as in "neighbor" and "weigh."
Examples: believe, receive.
Exceptions: height, either, conscience, financier.

5. For words ending in a single consonant and accented on the last syllable:
Double the final consonant before a suffix beginning with a vowel.
Examples: occur, occurred; control, controlled; begin, beginning.
Exceptions: bus, buses, gas, gaseous.

NOTES TO CHAPTER 9

(1) In a recent study conducted by a large high school, its graduates who were freshmen at many different colleges were asked which subject they considered the most difficult. English headed the list of courses mentioned. Over 80 per cent of the students felt they had trouble in written or oral expression. ("A Follow-Up Study of College Freshmen by a Secondary School," *Special Guidance Report,* No. 696, Chicago: Science Research Associates, 1962).

(2) English itself has about 175 "irregular" verbs according to C. C. Fries.

SUGGESTIONS FOR FURTHER READING

Arntson, Dorothy H., *Beginning College Writing.* Chicago: Scott, Foresman and Co., 1963.

Bloomfield, Leonard, *Outline Guide for the Practical Study of Foreign Languages.* Published by the Linguistic Society of America, Baltimore: Waverly Press, Inc., 1942.

Carter, Homer L. J. and Dorothy J. McGinnis, *Effective Reading for College Students.* New York: The Dryden Press, Inc., 1957.

Ciardi, John, *How Does a Poem Mean?* Boston: Houghton Mifflin, Co., 1959.

Cromwell, Harvey and Alan H. Monroe, *Working for More Effective Speech.* Chicago: Scott and Foresman and Co., 1964.

Gilbert, Doris W., *Power and Speed in Reading.* Englewood Cliffs, New Jersey: Prentice-Hall, Inc., 1956.

Glock, Marvin C., *The Improvement of College Reading*. Boston: Houghton Mifflin Co., 1954.

Johnston, Robert A. and John H. Link, *Improve Your Speech* (4th ed.). Chicago: The Cefalu Press, 1963.

Moulton, William G., *Study Hints for Language Students*. Boston: Houghton Mifflin Co., n.d.

CHAPTER 10

How Should You Study the Sciences?

Your success in studying the sciences depends mostly upon how well you understand basic principles and generalizations. When you understand a principle you can use it. You can see its applications under many conditions, and you can also recognize its limitations. *Understanding* thus requires more than just the repetition of words or formulas. Beware of memorizing without understanding.

Keep in mind that there are various levels of understanding which depend in part upon how well the learner uses his own experiences. When you are taught principles, try to think of your own examples. When you are taught facts, try to derive principles. In this way you can deepen your understanding.

WHAT IS SCIENCE?

In recent years there has been a great increase of public interest in science and a general feeling that we must "do something" about it. Unfortunately, this interest has not resulted in any great increase in public understanding of the content and method of science, nor has very much actually been done. A scientist, to the average man, is still a wild-haired, absent-minded genius in a white coat who putters among his mysterious bubbling glassware. Only recently have we begun to devote a fraction of the time and energy we spend on recruiting talented potential athletes to the recruiting and encouragement of talented potential scientists.

Let us begin our discussion of science by making a few simple distinctions. The term "science" should be restricted to a particular method of obtaining certain kinds of truths, the organization of these truths, and the logical inferences and generalizations which can be drawn from them. The sciences which deal with the living and nonliving universe are called, collectively, the *natural sciences;* those sciences which concentrate on man's association with other men are called the *social sciences.*

> *Science is the reduction of the bewildering diversity of unique events to manageable uniformity within . . . a . . . symbol [system], and technology is the art of using [this] symbol [system] so as to control and organize unique events . . . Education in science and technology is essentially education on the symbolic level.*
>
> **Aldous Huxley**

WHY SHOULD YOU STUDY NATURAL SCIENCES?

I had trouble with Phy Sci because I dislike the course and resented taking it when I'm not science-minded. I can not see the purpose behind making a Business Student take Phy Sci *or* Bi Sci.

A college freshman

To provide an answer as to why natural sciences are usually required of every college student, let us consider him as an individual, as a worker, and as a citizen of this country.

One of the objectives of every college is to produce an *educated individual.* Obviously, an educated individual must have some understand-

185

ing of the world around him, and science is an inescapable part of this world. The educated individual must be able to make intelligent decisions for himself on such common practical questions as whether or not he should smoke, what he should eat or drink, and what medications and immunizations he should undergo. In addition, he must be able to deal with the pseudo-scientific advertising and propaganda with which he is being continually bombarded by television, radio, and the press. The study of science can help with all of these problems and, in addition, furnish insights and methods which can be applied to many non-scientific questions as well.

The college student either is a *worker* or will be one. For the student who will earn his living as an engineer, farmer, technician, or scientist of some sort, his college science courses serve as direct preparation for his career. They will also furnish him with a background of theory to help illuminate his work. It was Einstein who remarked that nothing is as practical as a good theory. The student who will not earn his living in a scientific field may also find that what he has learned in science contributes to his understanding of his own occupation, whatever it may be. Finally, every college student ought to study the sciences because he is a *citizen*, and as a citizen he will be called upon to understand those scientific matters that affect the general public—nuclear testing, conservation of natural resources, fluoridation of water, control of drugs, space exploration—to mention only a few.

LEARNING NATURAL SCIENCES

Although science is a very modern subject, you will still have to do a lot of old-fashioned memorizing when you study it. Much of your memorizing will be devoted to the vocabulary of the science, a vocabulary made up partly of terms that will be new to you, and partly of ordinary words used in a special restricted sense. You may find that you are expected to learn as many new words in your science course as you learn in your language course. The easiest way to attack new science terms is by breaking them down into the parts or "roots" of which they are usually composed. If you will learn the meaning of each root as you go along, you will soon find that complicated new words often contain elements which are familiar to you. For example, if you encounter the formidable word, *"icthyophagous"* and if you know that the word *ichthyology* comes from the Greek *ichthys,* meaning "fish," and if you remember that *phagocyte* means "eating-cell," you can figure out the meaning of the unfamiliar word. For your convenience a list of common roots of scientific terms has been placed at the end of this chapter.

Be sure to use the pictures and diagrams provided by most science textbooks. They can help you to understand structures and processes. Whenever possible try to sketch illustrations from memory.

When your science courses require laboratory work, you must realize that such work is very time-consuming, and you must concentrate on working efficiently and accurately. One other word of caution about laboratory work—always draw or report your results precisely as you find them. It is both unwise and dishonest to tamper with experimental results in order to make them "look good."

Many freshmen are surprised to find that they must be exact when they express their ideas.

A college biology professor

Conclude your study of every topic by testing yourself. If you really understand, you will be able to solve the problems.

Levels of precision

In addition to learning the content of a science, you must also remember that you are dealing with a special method of learning truths. It is therefore necessary for you to know exactly how the information was obtained, and how accurate it is. Keep in mind that scientific truths may be available at various levels of precision. For example, take the question, "What is the shape of our planet, the earth?" You may think this question was settled a long time ago, but actually there is still a surprisingly wide variety of *true* answers available today. Let us examine some of the answers.

"The earth is flat"—This assumption is perfectly valid when dealing with small areas such as the site of a building.

"The earth is conical"—This approximation is good enough for dealing with the mapping of larger areas such as counties and states.

"The earth is round"—This is valid for the general purpose of visualizing the earth, as well as for some special purposes such as the navigation of ships and airplanes.

"The earth is an oblate spheroid"—This represents a slight refinement over the concept that the earth is perfectly spherical.

"The earth is slightly pear-shaped"—To the extent of less than one part in a thousand, the earth may depart from an ideal spheroid. This recent finding might be vital to the development of travel in space, but it would be irrelevant for most other uses.

In practice then, you may choose the answer you wish depending upon the purpose of the original question and the level of precision you require.

What is meant by scientific method?

The scientific method begins with the gathering of verified facts by a procedure we can summarize in six steps:

1) Stating a question or a problem.
2) Gathering background data on the question by "searching the literature" of the science.
3) Constructing a hypothesis or guess as to the correct answer.
4) Finding a procedure or experiment to test the hypothesis.
5) Using the procedure or performing the experiment. Results should be stated in numbers and should be repeatable, if possible. Lord Kelvin said, "*When you cannot measure it, when you cannot express it in numbers, your knowledge is of a meager and unsatisfactory kind*" (1).
6) Analyzing the results to determine whether the hypothesis is correct. Stating new questions.

As new facts or data are accumulated by these steps, there is an effort to explain them in the form of a general rule which will predict the results of future experiments. Such a generalization which explains all of the relevant facts is called a *theory*. Broad theories which have been found valid are sometimes called *principles* or *laws*. The main effort of scientists is toward *reducing the number of laws* which are needed to explain, predict, and control natural phenomena. For example, Newton's Three Laws of Motion served for many years to explain the results of centuries of experience with moving objects. More recently, these laws have been found to be inadequate to explain either the motions of the atoms or the motions of the stars. Einstein's theory of relativity is, in part, an attempt to include Newton's Laws as a special case within the more general laws which appear to govern the entire physical universe. Similarly, attempts are constantly being made to formulate more general biological laws which will include all the principles already known, in order to explain many of the phenomena of life.

WHAT ARE THE DIFFERENT SCIENCES?

There are many ways of classifying the sciences, and the older classifications are constantly being outdated by the founding of new interdisciplinary sciences. It is often convenient to divide the natural sciences into the **physical sciences** and the **biological** or **life, sciences.** Within the physical sciences we include physics, chemistry, geology, astronomy, and their many subdivisions. There are also such hybrid sciences as physical chemistry, astrophysics, and petrochemistry, to name a few.

Within the biological sciences we include those that concentrate on plants and those that concentrate on animals, as well as those that deal with micro-organisms. Each of these fields is still further divided according to the particular living group which is studied. Every group can be studied from the standpoint of its *functioning in* such disciplines as physiology, genetics, and ecology; or from the standpoint of its *structure* in such subjects as histology and anatomy.

To complete the picture, there is an increasing number of sciences which bridge the gap between the physical and the biological sciences such as mathematical biophysics, paleontology, and the biochemistry of the gene.

Finally, there is mathematics, which has been aptly characterized by E. T. Bell as "the queen and the servant of science."

LEARNING MATHEMATICS

Mathematics possesses not only truth, but supreme beauty—a beauty cold and austere, . . . sublimely pure, and capable of a stern perfection such as only the greatest art can show.

Bertrand Russell

Why should you study mathematics?

Everyone uses some form of mathematics every day of his life. We must all deal with precise quantities of time, distance, money, and goods of various sorts; indeed, we live in a mathematical world whether we realize it or not. The question of studying mathematics is therefore the question of whether or not we will carry on our necessary daily activities easily and accurately. Beyond our everyday lives, we find that a knowledge of mathematics is indispensable for an understanding of any science or any technology. For the gifted few, the intensive study of mathematics leads directly to many occupational fields which are in great demand today. The need for mathematicians in industry, government, and universities is increasing at a geometrical rate, to use a mathematical term.

Why is it that so many college students have difficulty with their courses in mathematics? The main reason, most likely, is that many freshmen enter college without certain *foundation skills* which are prerequisite to any further study. This lack of skill may be due to poor learning by the student during high school and elementary school. In turn, this may be traced partly to a common attitude that mathematics is dull, difficult, and burdensome. It cannot be denied that the teaching of mathematics, like the teaching of most other subjects, could be improved by greater stress on basic understanding and less on mere mechanical repetition. Nevertheless, learning must start from where the student is, and experience shows that it is possible for most college freshmen to make up their deficiencies in basic mathematical skills.

There is another reason for the difficulty some students experience in college mathematics: a lack of whatever it is that is measured by the *academic aptitude* tests, which usually provide a score for the ability to deal with quantities. Let us briefly consider the possible effects of receiving a low score in quantitative ability. You can let such a score discourage you completely, or you can regard it as one measure of how far you will have to go to bring yourself up to college standards in mathematics. Lack of mathematical ability as shown by your guidance tests should be a cause of serious concern to you but not a cause of panic, for it is your power to do something to improve your situation.

The first step is to find out what you can about the nature and extent of your problem. Then, if necessary, ask for help in setting up a reme-dial program for yourself. Probably the best method is to take a non-credit preparatory course in mathematics if your college offers one. Another good method is to obtain tutoring assistance on your specific problems. Or, instead, you may wish simply to study one or several of the various self-help or programmed learning texts in mathematics which are available today. This is a perfectly practical method, but it does take more self-discipline and perseverance than many freshmen seem to have.

> One must learn by doing the thing, for though you think you know it, you have no certainty until you try.
>
> Sophocles

How should mathematics be studied?

Begin studying mathematics as you begin studying anything else, by systematic reading. In the first reading you should try to get the *general idea* of what is being done and how it is related to what has gone before. Often, one reading is not enough and rereading is necessary. In later readings more attention should be given to *detail,* with the forces of your attention on *how* something is done and *why* it is done in a particular way. If you attempt to explain what you have read in your own words, it will help you to find the points which you do not understand. You can then go back over the text, paying particular attention to these points.

You will find *examples* particularly helpful in *understanding* the descriptive material. To get full benefit from examples, you must do more than just use them as models for assigned problems. First, ask yourself how the examples illustrate the descriptive material. If appropriate, draw a sketch or graph for yourself. When you think you understand the relationship between the examples and the descriptions in the text, try **making up examples** of your own. When you can do this, you are ready for the **practice** which will fix this particular process in your memory so you can use it with confidence whenever you need it. The understanding will enable you to decide when to apply the technique; the practice will enable you to apply it surely and efficiently. **Be sure that understanding comes before practice.** Merely trying to memorize formulas and rules which have no meaning for you is bound to be frustrating and unproductive.

> **The students report that the pace in college is much faster than in high school. This makes it imperative to keep up to date in class assignments. They find that once they fall behind in their math homework, it takes them two or three times as long to do the work.**
>
> **A mathematics professor**

Keep up with your assignments every day, whether or not your instructor grades or even collects them. Pay close attention in class and take notes. These notes should be an especially clear record of the explanations and illustrations given in class. They should be perfectly clear to you a day, a week, or even a month after you have written them.

Whenever you have the opportunity, be sure to **ask questions** about the point you do not understand. This may mean writing and underlining questions as you take your notes and as you read the text and do your assignments. Do not depend on your memory for this: Write the questions so that you will have them ready when the time comes to ask them. Sometimes by writing the question, you are able to focus on a particular difficulty so that you can answer the question yourself. A sharply defined question often brings out a brief and illuminating answer. A vague statement such as "I just don't know how to do these problems," may be followed by a long discussion in which the real difficulty gets only a small amount of attention.

Do not be afraid to ask questions. Generally, you will find that others want answers to the very questions you ask and are silent for fear of appearing stupid. It is far better to appear stupid in a question session and intelligent in the examination than to seem intelligent in such a session and stupid in the examination.

Begin your assigned work as soon as possible after each class meeting, but do not attempt to do problems before reading the text. If you can put together the class explanations and the descriptive material in your reviewing. If you find that you cannot overcome your difficulties, try to get help as soon as possible.

Suggestions for doing problems, particularly word problems

When doing problems in order to practice using techniques and applying principles, you must proceed in an orderly fashion. First, read the problem for general sense. Second, reread the problem with the following questions in mind:

> **What information is given?**
> **What am I trying to find?**
> **What are the relationships between the given and required information?**
> **How can I write these relationships symbolically?**
> **What operations must I use?**

It is surprising how many students will work furiously at a problem for some time and still be unable to answer the question, "What are you trying to find?"

After you have solved a problem, you should ask yourself one additional question: Is the answer reasonable? Before going on, you should be satisfied that your answer fulfills the conditions set forth in the problem.

What are the common errors to avoid?

The most common error of students in freshman mathematics courses is to be satisfied with a vague idea of how to work a particular problem. Later they discover to their astonishment that the slightest change in the form of the problem makes it impossible for them to solve.

> **A major problem of freshmen, I think, is the notion that doing regular work, having regular class attendance, and exuding good will will guarantee a passing grade. These students are often hurt when they discover that ability to solve the math problems is also essential.**
>
> **A mathematics instructor**

Surprisingly common also are errors in copying the problem and errors in simple arithmetic which we may call careless, but which students themselves sometimes refer to in stronger terms.

> **I haven't any real trouble in this course. I just keep on making these dumb stupid mistakes!**
>
> **A college freshman**

In order to avoid this kind of error, it is necessary to work more slowly and to form the habit of **checking your copying** of every problem as well as the arithmetic involved. In addition, check to make certain that your answer is stated in the *correct units* required by the problem.

The best way of avoiding ridiculous answers to practical problems is to begin by making a *shrewd guess* as to the correct answer. For example, if you have to calculate the square root of 32.654, you can easily guess that the answer will be between 5 and 6 because the square of 5 would be too little, and the square of 6 would be too much. Similarly, if you are making a chemical analysis and are figuring out how much reagent to add to your test tube, if your answer comes out in kilograms, you had better recheck your arithmetic. The practice of guessing the answer is particularly useful when using a slide rule or a table of logarithms.

All the various branches of mathematics make use of the same basic operations: addition, subtraction, multiplication, and division. Many common errors in elementary algebra result from a lack of understanding of these *basic operations and their inverses*. Addition and subtraction are inverse operations: each undoes what the other does. Multiplication and division are also inverse operations. You cannot "cancel" the 2's in $\dfrac{X+2}{2}$ since the 2 in the numerator is held in place by addition, while the 2 in the denominator indicates division by 2. **Addition is not "undone" by division.** On the other hand, $\dfrac{2(x-7)}{2}$ is equal to $(x-7)$ since the 2 in the numerator is a multiplier and the 2 in the denominator is a divisor, and **division "undoes" multiplication.**

Another common source of error in algebra lies in doing an operation which inadvertently *destroys an equality*. You should be very sure of what you can and cannot do if you wish to replace one equality by another related equality. This can be stated briefly in symbols as follows:

$$\text{If } A = B \text{ then}$$
$$A + C = B + C$$
$$A - C = B - C$$
$$A \cdot C = B \cdot C \text{ and}$$
$$\frac{A}{C} = \frac{B}{C} \text{ if C is not zero}$$

The main solution to the problem of avoiding errors in mathematics is to **analyze** your difficulties, **obtain help** to overcome them, and finally, **practice** enough to make your mastery secure.

LEARNING SOCIAL SCIENCES

Those who cannot remember the past are condemned to repeat it.
George Santayana

What are the social sciences? Modern man has made tremendous progress toward the control of his physical environment, but his efforts to build a better society lag far behind. Failures in human relations have led to personal tensions and disorders, to deviant and delinquent behavior, and to conflicts among men and among nations. We believe man's failures are due in large part to his ignorance about himself.

Social scientists seek to develop a science of society. They seek to understand, predict and control human relations. Their studies are based on the assumption that human behavior is not accidental, but the result of orderly and definable processes and forces, and that changes within the social system take place within certain sequences and according to certain laws. The social sciences have also been called the behavioristic sciences since they all deal with the way men behave in a social system.

John Maynard Keynes has pointed out that the social sciences affect all of us whether we know it or not: "Practical men, who believe themselves to be quite exempt from any intellectual influences, are usually the slaves of some defunct economist. Madmen in authority, who hear voices in the air, distill their frenzy from some academic scribbler of a few years back (2)."

Properly, the social sciences have these objectives:

1) To discover through research and experimentation the laws which regulate and control human behavior, and at the same time, to refine the tools of social observation and analysis.

2) To test and evaluate the current theories and popular beliefs about human relations, and to provide liberation from cultural biases and prejudices toward other people and their ways of life. Studies indicate that understanding people whose folkways are different usually leads to better human relations between people.

3) To provide all men with knowledge and understanding of society so that they may more fully understand themselves, and that they may have an adequate base for intelligent, self-directed, imaginative living.

There have been a number of significant changes in the field of social science in the past several years, including the following:

1) There is an increasing awareness of the inadequacy of human reason by itself. This has led to a greater stress on objective observation and experimentation. Students are encouraged to leave their classroom and use the world with all of its real-life situations as their laboratory.

2) Emphasis has shifted from particular social problems to the general description and measurement of all social facts. Studies go beyond concentration on race relations, juvenile delinquency, poverty, and mental illness, for example.

3) Little effort is made to define what is wrong with society, and still less effort to imagine what society ought to be. Instead, the social scientist describes society as it exists, and determines the direction of the various changes which are taking place.

4) Interest in tests and measurements has increased and there is greater enthusiasm for statistics and mathematical formulas. Beginning students sometimes rebel at the number of formulas, charts, and tables found in the professional writings. Yet they must realize that mathematics is the language of every science.

What are the major divisions of the social sciences?

Anthropology is the study of man and his society, with reference to both biological and cultural aspects.

Economics is the study of how people go about making a living.

Geography is the study of man's dependency upon the physical environment and the adaptation of his social system to its requirements.

History is the study of man's past and the events that have shaped the structure and character of the world today. "Study antiquity," said Pope John XXIII, "to find the key to the present."

Political Science is the study of government and the forms of formal social control.

Psychology is the science of individual behavior. Often, it is also considered an aspect of the biological sciences.

Sociology is the study of the basic structures of society and the factors that are involved in the strengthening and weakening of the social order.

In addition, there are a number of interdepartmental fields such as **Social Psychology, Political Geography, Human Development, Educational Sociology, Sociology of Religion,** and so on, which combine the materials and methods of two or more special areas.

How should you study the social sciences?

Most students come to the social science classroom with a number of values and beliefs concerning the nature of man and the characteristics of a good society. In the class they are required to examine these values and beliefs and to evaluate them objectively in the light of the findings of social science. Sometimes a student is reluctant to accept facts that do not agree with what he thought either existed or ought to exist in society. Occasionally, a student may experience some anxiety and insecurity and may react by attacking the teacher and the subject matter. A more intelligent reaction is to use the class work as a basis for testing one's own beliefs, rebuilding them on the basis of new insights, or discarding them when they are no longer tenable. Sometimes a previously cherished belief is lost temporarily but comes back when it is supported by deeper understandings instead of rote learnings.

Social science courses stress critical thinking and the understanding of general concepts rather than the mere accumulation of a series of facts. Frequently, examinations test the student's ability to apply the concepts to new situations and new materials.

It is sometimes said that as a relatively new field of serious study, social science has not yet had sufficient time to refine its methods and its materials. A student should therefore be prepared to confront a wide variety of opinions and even considerable changes in accepted theories from time to time. Because the tools of social science do not have the precision and accuracy of other sciences, students often labor under the delusion that the mastery of social science is easy. They are likely to find that social science courses are rarely "snap" courses.

> **I've had most of my trouble in social science. I would read the chapter very thoroughly but when I took the test I did not do well. The questions would seem familiar and I thought I knew the answers but I guess I didn't.**
>
> **A college freshman**

Always remember that human behavior is very complex. We act in response to a whole galaxy of causes and effects, most of which we do not understand clearly. Students should therefore avoid the common tendency to seek glib simplifications and comfortable generalizations.

Finally, despite the difficulties which are inherent in studying the social sciences, keep in mind that unless we can solve the basic social problem of how to live in peace with each other, nothing else we study will be of very much importance in the future.

NOTES TO CHAPTER 10

(1) Cited by Bernard Berelson and Gary A. Steiner, *Human Behavior* (New York: Harcourt, Brace and World, Inc.), 1964.

(2) *Ibid.*

Common Roots Of Scientific Terms

ROOT	DERIV.	MEANING
A, an	Grk.	without
Actin	Grk.	radiation, ray
Ad	Lat.	to, toward
Aer	Grk.	air
Andr	Grk.	man, male
Annu, annul	Lat.	ring-shaped
Ante	Lat.	before
Anth	Grk.	flower
Anthr	Grk.	human
Anti	Lat.	against
Apic	Lat.	top, upper end
Arch	Grk.	early, first
Argent	Lat.	silver
Arthr	Grk.	joint
Aster, astr	Grk.	star
Aur	Lat.	gold
Bi	Lat.	two or twice
Brev	Lat.	short
Bucc	Lat.	cheek
Card	Grk.	heart
Cata, catha	Grk.	downward, outward
Cel, coel	Grk.	cavity
Chlor	Grk.	green
Chrom	Grk.	color
Circ	Lat.	around
Cis	Lat.	this side of
Co, com, con	Lat.	with, together
Cord	Lat.	heart
Cran	Lat.	skull
Crypt	Grk.	hidden
Cum	Lat.	with, together
Cupr	Lat.	copper
Cyan	Grk.	blue, blue-green
Cyst	Grk.	bladder
Cyt	Grk.	cell
Deca	Grk.	ten

Common Roots Of Scientific Terms (Continued)

ROOT	DERIV.	MEANING
Demi	Grk.	half
Dens, dent	Lat.	tooth
Derm	Grk.	skin
Deutero	Grk.	secondary
Dexter, dextr	Lat.	right-hand
Di	Grk.	twice
Dia	Grk.	across
Diplo	Grk.	paired
Dors	Lat.	upper or back side
Dyn	Grk.	energy, force
Echin	Grk.	spiny
Eco	Grk.	house, habitat
Ecto	Grk.	outer
Ectomy	Grk.	removal by surgery
En	Grk.	in
Endo, ento	Grk.	inner
Enter	Grk.	intestine
Epi	Grk.	upon
Erg	Grk.	energy, work
Erythro	Grk.	red
Eu	Grk.	true, good
Ex	Lat.	out
Exo	Lat.	outer
Extra	Lat.	outside of
Fer	Lat.	bear, put
Ferr	Lat.	iron
Flor	Lat.	flower
Fol	Lat.	leaf
Gastr	Grk.	stomach
Gen	Grk.	birth, origin
Geo	Grk.	earth
Gon	Grk.	reproductive body
Gyn	Grk.	female
Haplo	Grk.	half
Helio	Grk.	sun
Helminth	Grk.	worm
Hemi	Grk.	half
Hepta	Grk.	seven
Heter	Grk.	other
Hexa	Grk.	six
Holo	Grk.	entire

Common Roots Of Scientific Terms (Continued)

ROOT	DERIV.	MEANING
Homin	Lat.	human
Homo	Lat.	man
Homo, homeo	Grk.	same
Hydr	Grk.	water
Hyper	Grk.	excessive
Idio	Grk.	individual
Ichthy	Grk.	fish
In	Lat.	in, into
In	Lat.	not
Inter	Lat.	between
Iso	Grk.	similar, equal
Kata	Grk.	down, out
Kin	Grk.	energy
Lamin	Lat.	blade or layer
Later	Lat.	side
Leuco	Grk.	white, milky
Levulo	Lat.	left-hand
Logy	Grk.	word, discourse, teaching, science
Long	Lat.	long
Lux, luc	Lat.	light
Macr	Grk.	large
Max	Lat.	most, highest
Mega	Grk.	large
Melan	Grk.	dark, black
Mens	Lat.	measure, month
Meta	Grk.	middle
Micr	Grk.	small
Minim	Lat.	least, lowest
Mon	Grk.	one
Morph	Grk.	form, shape
Mult	Lat.	many
My	Grk.	muscle
Myc	Grk.	fungus
Nema	Grk.	thread
Neur	Grk.	nerve
Nom	Lat.	name
Nomic, nomy	Grk.	conduct, management
Ob	Lat.	inverted
Octa	Lat., Grk.	eight
Ombr	Lat.	shade

Common Roots Of Scientific Terms (Continued)

ROOT	DERIV.	MEANING
Ophth	Grk.	eye
Oö	Grk.	egg
Ortho	Grk.	straight
Ovo	Lat.	egg
Pal, palae, pale	Grk.	old, ancient
Pan	Grk.	all
Para	Grk.	beside
Parthen	Grk.	virgin
Path	Grk.	suffer
Pen, pend	Lat.	attached to
Penta	Grk.	five
Per	Lat.	through
Phaeno	Grk.	showing, visible
Phag	Grk.	eat, devour
Phil	Grk.	loving
Phob	Grk.	hating
Phot	Grk.	light
Phyc	Grk.	alga, sea weed
Phyl	Grk.	leaf
Phyt	Grk.	plant
Pisc	Lat.	fish
Plasm, plasma	Grk.	substance
Plat	Grk.	flat
Pneum	Grk.	wind, air
Pod	Grk.	foot
Poly	Grk.	many
Post	Lat.	after
Pre	Lat.	before
Prim	Lat.	first
Prot	Grk.	first, earliest
Pseud	Grk.	false
Pter	Grk.	wing, feather
Quadr	Lat.	four
Quint	Lat.	five
Radic	Lat.	root
Rect	Lat.	in a straight line
Rhod	Grk.	red, rose-colored
Schiz	Grk.	split
Scop	Grk.	see, look
Semi	Lat.	half
Septa	Lat.	seven

Common Roots Of Scientific Terms (Continued)

ROOT	DERIV.	MEANING
Sexa	Lat.	six
Sol	Lat.	sun
Som, soma	Grk.	body
Spec	Lat.	visible, showy
Stear, steat	Grk.	fat
Stel	Lat.	star
Stele	Grk.	column
Stoma	Grk.	mouth
Styl	Grk.	pillar
Sub	Lat.	under, less than
Super, supra	Lat.	above, over
Sym, syn	Grk.	together
Tax	Grk.	arrangement
Taxy	Grk.	movement
Tele	Grk.	distant, last
Ter	Grk.	three
Tetra	Grk.	four
Tom, tomy	Grk.	cut
Tor	Lat.	crooked
Tox	Grk.	poison
Trans	Lat.	beyond, across
Tri	Lat.	three
Trop	Grk.	turn
Ult	Lat.	last
Umbr	Lat.	shade
Uni	Lat.	one
Uri	Grk.	tail
Vent	Lat.	lower or belly side
Virg	Lat.	rod, wand
Xanth	Grk.	yellow
Zoö, zoa	Grk.	animal

HAPPINESS IS HAVING STUDIED FOR THE RIGHT EXAM AT THE RIGHT TIME —

CHAPTER 11

Can You Do Better on Examinations?

Examinations are an extremely important part of your college work. They are the major method of determining your course grades and, as more colleges encourage independent study programs, comprehensive examinations may come to replace in-course evaluations. Even after you leave college, you may have to face examinations again when applying for a job with a large corporation or trying to enter some form of civil service.

Tests can be an important educational experience in themselves. They generally force you to review your previous work and organize your thoughts. Some examinations also require you to express yourself clearly and forcefully.